# Friendly Persuasion

---

## Dynamic Telephone Sales Training and Techniques for the 21st Century

---

## Dan Coen

# CONTENTS

Design by Graphics One, Northridge, CA

Edited by Marie Burkenheim

This publication is published with the understanding that the publisher and
author are not engaged in rendering legal advice.

Library of Congress Catalog Card Number: 97-94528
ISBN 0- 9660436 - 1- 8

**❝**

Well organized and informative. The original concepts in <u>Friendly Persuasion</u> take the art of selling to a whole new level.

**❞**

*Wayne Hoyt, Executive Recruiter*

**❝**

The communication approaches Dan Coen teaches between radio, sports and telephone selling truly enlighten the reader. His theories about listening, hearing and closing sales are outstanding!

**❞**

*Bill Burton, Program Director, KTFN Radio, 1580*

**❝**

<u>Friendly Persuasion</u> should be the foundation of any call center. Very well developed and concise, this book has helped me tremendously in the training of my sales reps.

**❞**

*Howard Nehdar, Sales Director, Hummingbird Communications*

**❝**

After reading <u>Friendly Persuasion</u>, I found myself armed with dozens of ideas for training and motivating my sales force. This book is a treasure.

**❞**

*Clarence McDowell, Tele-Sales Director, The St. John Companies*

**❝**

Take note sales trainers and managers! A brilliant outline providing specific action plans and demonstrating clear step-by-step formulas. A fantastic study of the art of communication and sales, this is a must for coaches, managers and trainers.

**❞**

*Matt Borchert, Head Women's Basketball Coach, Gavilan College*

❝ This book spells out comprehensive Telemarketing concepts in a notably readable manner. Every inbound or outbound call center will benefit from the successful hands-on examples of selling, persuasion and communication. ❞

*Deb Shaul, Call Center Consultant*

# Introduction

The telephone is such a common part of modern life that it is inconceivable for most of us to imagine a day without it. Take a look at your fellow workers, business associates, friends and family members. Whether they spend their time on the phone conducting business, gossiping relentlessly or zipping along in their cars on the freeway, their actions make it clear that the telephone has become the instrument of choice and convenience in our society. Today, people from all over can't remember a time when the telephone didn't exist and didn't impact the way they communicate with others; that time so long ago when communication meant mail or personal contact, and required loads of patience. With new technologies such as fax, the Internet and e-mail, the telephone has gone from a miracle that has changed the world, to a mainstay in society that propels the world to even greater heights.

Still, with all of the people who have used the telephone in the last hundred years, only a few actually have mastered the telephone as a powerful selling and communications tool. What do I mean by powerful? Well, from the first telephone call, people have always used it to communicate with one another, but few understood the dynamic intricacies of that communication and how it could be improved upon. Each party talked to (or at) the other without realizing the ways in which they were impacting the responses they received. It is important to recognize that what we say on the telephone motivates others to make decisions. This is powerful! Simply stated, people are motivated to act and react through the dialogue they receive and through the dialogue they produce. Communication, whether friendly persuasion or not, is a form of selling, as is selling a form of communication. Yet, for the last hundred years a true understanding of the ways in which this incredible selling and communications tool can change the world has not been recognized.

This book provides a comprehensive, in-depth examination of the telephone as a modern tool of communication for people who use the telephone day-in and day-out. I focus this book on the sales world because I am a believer in the philosophy that all communication is sales, aggressive or not, soft sell or not. Nevertheless, although the focus of this book is on the sales world, reality dictates that this book is all about powerful communications, not just sales as we think of sales. For example, whether the reader is preparing to begin a casual telephone call or actually to sell and persuade via the telephone, this book will help him to obtain a better understanding of how he can use the telephone to communicate, sell and achieve results in the modern world of the 21st century. From beginning to end, hundreds of topics are explored in an easy-to-follow format so that novices, telephone sales representatives, students, sales managers, educators, and any person fascinated by the art of person-to-person interaction can learn the techniques, pitfalls, and concepts of telephone sales and communications.

Because the sales close is such an important facet of any dynamic telephone sales presentation, every chapter of this book concentrates on skills which lead the TSR to the close. In addition, each chapter builds a foundation for the reader, until the last chapters are reached, where closing sales are highlighted. For that reason, any chapter can be read independently of the others, or the book can be read sequentially in order to explore the intricate workings of a sales presentation.

Although I teach that closing is, of course, important and I agree wholeheartedly in its importance, my view is that there are two elements of telephone selling that are much more important then the close, and that TSRs must recognize, learn and understand these elements if they are to succeed on the telephone. In fact, it is my belief that everything a telephone sales presentation is can be condensed into two dynamic skill-sets that always make or break a presentation and a close. These skill-sets consist of LISTENING and HEARING.

The main theme of this book is that listening to and hearing what customers and prospects are saying is the missing link to telephone sales and communications. TSRs must understand that customers will be more approachable, and therefore more sellable, if they have first been convinced that the TSR is available to serve them. This act of being available is effectuated by listening.

Similarly, it is universally agreed that understanding what a customer wants is an important step toward closing a sale. If the TSR comprehends what the customer wants, he has a better chance of delivering what that customer wants. To understand what a customer wants, the TSR must hear what the customer is saying.

Listening and Hearing are different skill-sets. They involve different disciplines, and they eventually affect the customer in different ways. Listening encourages the customer to continue communicating, and listening develops relationship. Hearing involves understanding what customers need and what customers want, and how customers can best be sold. Hence, this book takes as its theme the three topics that we have just discussed—closing, listening and hearing.

# APPLYING LISTENING AND HEARING TO TELEPHONE SELLING

By listening to a customer, the TSR is providing him with strict attention. Persuading a customer that the TSR is listening intently to his issues and concerns is a step toward gaining the customer's trust and establishing a comfortable relationship. This trust is an important factor in setting up the customer for the close.

Listening skills involve verbal nods that let the customer know that the TSR is involved in the conversation:

"Uh huh."

"Really."

"No kidding."

"Keep going."

"Wow."

"Ummm."

"How interesting."

Effective listening promotes relationship-building. It is amazing to see how many customers credit the TSR with credibility strictly because the TSR listens to them. (Senior citizens alone in the home, parents with concerns about their child's education, young adults interested in a particular course of study, single adults leading a busy lifestyle.) Almost every individual wants someone to listen to him, and reacts positively when someone does.

Listening opens a plethora of opportunities for the TSR. Listening forges a relationship with the customer that will go a long way toward closing the sale when the time is right.

Hearing what the customer is trying to say places a TSR miles ahead in the race to the close, because customers often have difficulty expressing themselves. Hearing all the details of what a customer is saying is the path toward discovering the information necessary to close the sale. Hearing what the customer is really saying allows the TSR to figure out exactly what the customer wants and needs.

For example, what is a customer saying when he says he can't afford the product? Does he really lack money, in which case the TSR failed to properly qualify him, or is he using the lack of money as an excuse to end the conversation? Or is the customer under a mistaken impression as to the cost of the product? A TSR who has heard the customer from the beginning will be able to decipher the real connotations to the customer's statements, and will therefore be able to respond (act and react) properly.

## CONDITIONING – THE STUMBLING BLOCK TO SUCCESS

The arts of listening and hearing both involve acting and reacting. When a pedestrian hears warning bells at a railroad crossing, he acts and reacts. When someone in an argument hears statements by the other party, he also acts and reacts. Successful listening and hearing have much to do with societal conditioning. In our society, listening and hearing are two of the traits we find most difficult to master. Perhaps this is due to the rushed manner in which we live our lives. Who has time to listen and hear? Who has the concentration and focus to listen and hear when our minds are cluttered with so many different things?

The inability to truly listen and hear causes us difficulty in many situations—with friends, family, business associates, peers and subordinates. Often, we attempt to communicate, but we don't accumulate information or assimilate it. For example, we may hear a report on a news or talk radio station (or at least we think we're hearing it!), and then not remember, two minutes later, anything the newscaster or radio personality said. (i.e. Did the sportscaster say our team won the game? Did the woman in the helicopter say there was an accident on this freeway or on another one?)

The failure to listen and hear often extends to our personal lives as well. We might sit at the dinner table for two hours and talk with a group of people, only to come away with no understanding of or gain from the conversation. In some ways, society has conditioned us not to relate.

TSRs, as members of our society, are subject to the above-described weaknesses. When on the telephone, TSRs must fight this conditioning every time they make a presentation. The TSR's ability to truly listen and hear becomes crucial because a TSR's success or failure at work depends on his mastery of these skills.

## SUMMARY OF LISTENING AND HEARING SKILLS

Without using the dual skills of listening and hearing, the TSR will find that his sales presentations generally will result in failure.

The skills of listening and hearing are different from one another, and they are learned. The TSR must focus in order to put these skills to use.

The traits needed to perfect the skills of listening and hearing include focusing, practicing, perceiving and communicating.

The TSR must listen to exactly what the customer is saying and provide him with verbal nods so the customer understands that his thoughts count.

With every customer comment, the TSR must HEAR those points that the customer is attempting to make.  Not only must the words be heard, but their real meaning must be grasped and the reasons why the customer is making them must be figured out.

The TSR must formulate a response that demonstrates to the customer that he has been listening to the customer's comments, and hearing what the customer means.

It is my hope to help make individuals and organizations successful when they sell and communicate via the telephone.  Always remember that the sales power of the telephone is a dynamic force.  What you say and how you say it will motivate other people's actions.  I welcome any comments or questions and, as always, I promise I will listen to and hear each and every one of them.

Dan Coen
Los Angeles, California
November, 1998

*To Mom, Dad, Computers and the Public Library.*
*Each impacted my life in too many ways.*

*To Myrna and Debbie.*
*You taught me why the telephone is so popular.*

# CHAPTER 1

## ADVANTAGES AND DISADVANTAGES OF TELEPHONE SELLING

I was with my good friend donating much too much money to a thriving casino in Las Vegas when he asked me if the job of selling over the telephone is a limiting job. "What do you mean?" I asked. "Well, it seems so difficult to communicate aspects of a program and market products over the telephone and actually be successful at it. I don't understand why people think it can be done, and why people would want to do it. I don't see any advantages to it."

My friend's view is quite common outside of the telephone sales industry, and I am certain that my friend is not the first high level executive to feel that way about the industry of telephone selling. I played a couple more hands of cards, thinking about his comments, and thinking what the best ways would be to convince him how truly extraordinary communicating and marketing over the telephone is. Finally, I knew what to say.

"Read Chapter One in my book."

In all facets of sales, every sales person utilizes two communication tools. I simply call these communication tools visuals and verbals. Within telephone sales, visuals as we know them exist, but only when it comes to certain descriptive tactics, as we will explore in more detail in the next chapter. In this respect, verbals are required to be twice as powerful in order to make sales happen, because verbals are what telephone selling encompasses. When the TSR communicates with the customer, the TSR's **advantage** is that he may think of himself strictly as a verbalizing machine about 95% of the time. On the other hand, every time the TSR communicates with the customer, the TSR's disadvantage is that he doesn't have traditional visuals to assist him in closing sales.

The true study of telephone selling only dates back the last thirty years or so, and most folks feel that telephone selling really blossomed back in the late 1970's. It was with the advent of technology, particularly computer systems and dialing enhancements, that telephone selling became an accepted professional career, because technology increased opportunities. Hence, the term "telemarketing" has come into play only in the past 20 years, and it has been only during the past fifteen years that modern thought on selling over the telephone has been developed. In essence, I am a strong proponent of the theory that the study of telephone selling today is at the same stage as was the production of television commercials in the 1960's. Today, the study of telephone sales is good, as were commercials in the 1960's. But look at the advancement, in terms of creativity and depth, of television commercials. Today, technology has increased creativity, and commercials have become a much larger selling machine all their own. For example, I think back to those "Bud Bowls" commercials that always appeared during each Super Bowl. Also, even smaller budgeted commercials can utilize technology extensively to produce a quality, and entertaining, product. In this sense, the future of telephone selling is wide open, and has great opportunities to change immeasurably. But, we have a long way to go.

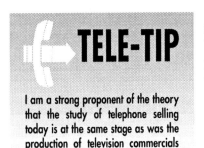

I am a strong proponent of the theory that the study of telephone selling today is at the same stage as was the production of television commercials in the 1960's.

For decades, little thought was given to the advantages and disadvantages of selling over the telephone versus other forms of selling. For so long, habit dictated that sales were done "door-to-door" in a personal style that provided comfort to the customer, so telephone selling wasn't even considered to be a true selling medium. With door-to-door selling, the customer could relax at home, meet his salesperson, and view the product in action. With the growth of technological communications, selling immediately began to be designed for the mediums of radio, television and mail. Still, telephone selling was never considered a strong, sturdy option.

Hence, most TSRs begin their jobs with little or no background on the advantages and disadvantages of selling over the telephone. Think about why this doesn't bode well for the industry. How can somebody profess to make his career in telephone selling if he can't, on the spur of the moment, list the reasons telephone selling is advantageous to him? Similarly, how can he make a career of selling over the telephone if he isn't honest with himself about the disadvantages of telephone selling?

Taking this into account, below are the six primary advantages to selling over the telephone and choosing telephone selling as a career. These advantages are the reasons people are going to say "yes" to TSRs over the telephone. They are the reasons customers will feel comfortable with the telephone sales presentation. And they are the reasons why so many telephone sales professionals find satisfaction in their jobs.

### 1. Customers Enjoy the Convenience of Talking over the Telephone

This is the same reason why customers enjoy purchasing products from the Internet and home shopping channels. It's easy, simple and can be done in the luxury of one's own home.

### 2. Customers Feel Comfortable Using the Telephone

This was certainly not true in the past. In the past, the telephone was only a social tool. But today business is done over the telephone quite often, and that makes the telephone a more credible instrument than it used to be – even when the customer is at home; especially when the customer is at work.

### 3. Customers Equate the Telephone to Social Interaction

This advantage of selling over the telephone relies completely on the TSR's ability to create an intimate conversation. We usually spend creative and fulfilling time on the telephone with people we enjoy speaking with. Hence, if the customer enjoys speaking with the TSR, he begins to think of the TSR more in the light of "friend" than "salesperson". A customer can't see the TSR, so the TSR's skill in developing this friendship will keep the customer's mind actively away from the fact that the TSR is selling.

### 4. A TSR May Be As Comfortable As He Wishes

The telephone provides a hidden element of surprise. In our society it is accurate to state that people judge other people by what they wear and how they look – the telephone eliminates this form of decision making by putting the customer in a position of trust. The telephone sales rep can be wearing a full three - piece suit surrounded by a 1500 square foot office, or he can wear ripped jeans and a T-shirt and be calling from his living room. In either arena, the customer must trust that the telephone sales rep is legitimate and worth his while to talk to. Very few customers will say "yes" to an offer from a person who is considered to be less of an authority regarding the product, or less friendly, than acceptable. By selling over the telephone, the telephone sales rep is in his most comfortable position, and does not need to worry about any preconceived biases from the customer. His only job is to attempt to fit the type of mold the customer is hoping he fits into.

### 5. A TSR Can Have All His Information Available

Selling over the telephone is somewhat like taking an open-book exam. The telephone sales rep has all his information available to him at all times, and can use this information in any way he chooses without the risk of appearing unprepared. For example, the telephone sales rep can have a sheet of paper on how to close the sale sitting on one side of his desk, a sheet on what the best benefits of the program are on the other, and a list of answers to the most commonly asked questions in the middle. The telephone sales rep prepares at his speed in his surroundings, and can use this to his advantage. On the contrary, selling in person puts the sales person right on the spot. He cannot move around and fish for notes too often or he will look unprepared; he cannot ask his boss a question because his boss is miles away, rather than standing right behind him. By selling over the phone, the telephone sales rep has all the information he needs within a three-foot radius (his desk) and he can access this information at any time.

## 6. A TSR Can Be Both Artist and Actor

Becoming an actor over the telephone is quite easy, and it lets the customer imagine who the sales person is on the other end. In addition, putting on a show over the phone is a fantastic way to make sales, because much of selling derives from showmanship. I once worked with a telephone sales rep who every other day would make a few sales calls sounding exactly like the late actor Jimmy Stewart. He did this because he could do a superb imitation of Stewart, but he also did it because the customers invariably were entertained by the call and became comfortable enough to tell this telephone sales rep that he <u>sounded like Jimmy Stewart</u>. "Why thank-thank-thank you, you, you," the telephone sales rep would reply.

There is no reason why the customer should not think that the TSR is the president of his company calling to sell him something. The customer should wonder if the TSR is tall or short, attractive, educated, standing or sitting. The customer should wonder who the TSR is and what the TSR does after work; he should realize that indeed the TSR does have something to do in this world other than to sell him a product, and he should be curious about the TSR just as the telephone sales rep is curious about him. It is true that the more times a customer questions the TSR about something (especially if that question has nothing to do with the actual sale of the product) the more likely the TSR is going to be able to close the sale, because he has actively involved the customer in the telephone call . By being able to make himself out to be whatever way he wants to be over the telephone, the TSR has the golden opportunity to create the **SUPER SALESPERSON** without running the risk of being considered a fraud or a phony. Friends may see the TSR as "Rick" or "Donna", but over the telephone the TSR can become anything he wishes to be. By using his voice and personality and the mystery of telephone selling as a weapon, the telephone sales rep can dominate a sales presentation by gathering the customer's trust and curiosity.

Telephone selling is, of course, a dangerous medium for the potential customer. Fraud charges against those not-so-friendly call centers are at an all time high, and this damages everybody in the industry. Below are six very important reasons why there are severe disadvantages to selling over the telephone, and why choosing a career in telephone selling can be a difficult choice. Perhaps this list is more important to the TSR than the first list of advantages, because this list allows the TSR to comprehend exactly why customers may not be receptive to his calls.

### 1. Customers Are Conditioned Not To Accept Telephone Solicitations

This is the major disadvantage when selling over the telephone. Society and the media have portrayed telephone selling in such a negative light that it has become incredibly difficult to convince a customer of the merits of the telephone call.

**TELE-TIP**

The vacuum cleaner salesperson would have a much more difficult time selling a vacuum over the telephone than in person for the simple reason that he would not be able to demonstrate the benefits of the vacuum.

### 2. Customers Don't Have the Time or Energy to Be Solicited

Let's face it. The reality is that there is never, and will never, be a good time for a customer to be sold. There may be a good time for a customer to listen, and there may be a good time for a customer to say "yes" to an offer, but customers are people, and people have many factors that play out in their lives. Most of those factors tend to occur right when a TSR is calling.

### 3. Customers Don't Want To Make Decisions Over The Telephone

Any selling encounters the problem of decision making, but it seems that telephone selling encounters it consistently. Because of the distance that exists between TSR and customer, customers don't feel pressured or motivated to make decisions. How bothersome is a TSR who constantly calls to ask a customer to make a decision? Bothersome, but not successful.

### 4. Customers Are Unable To See The TSR – A Credibility Problem

Comfort level over the telephone is a very difficult thing to achieve with a customer who does almost all of his business in person. Our society is designed so that we enter into transactions and make decisions with people we see and know in some fashion, not through conversations with strangers. Many customers want personal contact with their sales people and that reassures them that their decisions will be correct. Almost all customers are leery of agreeing to an order over the telephone without seeing the TSR. Before they will make a decision these people need to believe that the TSR is just like them and not some crazy looking "sales monster" hoping to steal their life savings. Most people find it difficult to say "yes" to a sales person anyway, so they find it even more difficult to say "yes" when they cannot look a telephone sales rep in the eye, or touch that TSR's shoulder, or shake that TSR's hand.

## 5. Customers Are Unable To See The Product

People tend to buy what they see, and selling over the telephone takes this option completely away. For example, in today's age, people commonly believe what they see. They believe what they see on television or read in the papers or see for themselves, and have trouble believing what they cannot see. The vacuum cleaner salesperson would have a much more difficult time selling a vacuum over the telephone than in person for the simple reason that he would not be able to demonstrate the benefits of the vacuum. Since the customers would not be able to see the vacuum and compare it to their present one, the salesman would be placed at a great disadvantage. This is why many customers want to see "something in the mail". They want "something faxed" before they make a decision. Perhaps the most irritating request a telephone sales rep receives on his sales calls is the request to "see something in writing." The biggest drawback to making sales over the telephone is that no matter how skilled the TSR is at painting a picture about his product, customers will be hesitant to say "yes" until they can see his product. This is why many telephone sales companies offer risk free trials, preview packages and money back guarantees. They understand that a straight buy is less appealing to a customer than one with an escape should the customer find that the product is not everything it was claimed to be. If the customer trusts the telephone sales rep, the rep has a chance to sell the product based almost entirely on the basis of that relationship, but if the customer wants some proof of the truth of what the telephone sales rep is saying , then the inability to view the product beforehand is a dilemma which catches telephone sales reps all the time.

## 6. Customers Are Unable To Provide Full Attention

It is no secret that if the telephone sales representative does not have the customer's attention, he will not get the customer interested in the sell. Many times we talk to people and think they are listening when in fact they are not paying attention to the telephone call at all. For example, when selling in person, if the customer isn't giving the sales rep full attention the sales rep will be cognizant of the fact that the sale is not going well, and take steps to remedy that. But over the phone the customer is just as able to avoid listening, as he is able to listen. Unless the TSR actively involves the customer with basic selling techniques such as trial closes and questions, the customer may put down the phone and eat a sandwich, read or watch television, or pay little attention to what is being said as he thinks of a way to get off the phone politely. In many instances customers simply take the phone and lay it on a desk while the TSR is selling, never to return again. Over the telephone, the TSR's personality and ability to present the product in an interesting fashion will be his only tools to utilize to gain the customer's full attention.

# CHAPTER  2

## UNDERSTANDING
## TELEPHONE SELLING

Thousands of TSRs don't understand telephone selling, and this lack of understanding limits their potential to make money. It also sets back the industry. I don't believe that TSRs are entirely at fault in this respect. Certainly, people are accountable for their own choices, and in that respect they are at fault. Yet, little formal time has been spent teaching the industry and the medium to TSRs, and this lack of scholarship means that TSRs haven't been given the opportunity to learn. My experiences have been that TSRs know they are required to sell, but they don't know *why* they succeed when they sell, or *how* they succeed when they sell, or *why* some selling techniques work and others don't. In addition, they don't understand *why* one customer reacts a certain way to a telephone sales presentation while another customer reacts a different way. Some TSRs succeed, others fail, but in any event, few of them know why.

I once gathered together six non-TSRs and asked them what they thought of telephone selling. To no surprise of mine, they each came back with the same response, worded differently. Each conveyed a lack of respect for and understanding of the industry. "No" I exclaimed, "Telephone selling involves much more than simply sitting in a chair enjoying a soft drink. It is much more fascinating than that." Unfortunately, this image, and many images like this one, are the predominant views of telephone selling and of TSRs. (i.e. it's a lazy job, anybody can do it, the folks who do it are quite unspectacular, and most telephone calls are bothersome scams that no honest minded individual would want to become involved with anyhow.) Between TSRs who don't understand their own industry and novices who have preconceived notions of the industry, it is no surprise that many people just don't understand telephone selling.

Here is a more honest assessment. Telephone selling is clearly a professional occupation, and a TSR's position involves serious dedication as well as a clever mixture of psychology and emotions. If the TSR can use psychology and emotions to his advantage, he will capture the centerpiece of successful selling over the telephone and in turn impact the way society views TSRs. The reason many TSRs don't excel in their profession, and the reason customers feel telephone selling and TSRs aren't on the "up and up" when they solicit, is because telephone selling isn't viewed by TSRs as a psychological and emotional medium. Too many TSRs think they are just performing another job.

## TELE-TIP

Telephone selling is an emotional industry, and customers react positively when they are emotionally motivated to do so.

This brings me to that well-known and often repeated story about the three men building a temple in the middle of the desert. Generations of men, family after family, began the process of building this temple. Those who began the process of building the temple had long passed away when their children's children finally completed the project. On the first day of this project, each man had been asked what he was building. The first man said, "I'm building a temple". The second man said, "I'm building a temple". The third man said, "I'm building a great temple which will be the largest in the world, a Mecca for centuries of civilizations to learn from and enjoy."

Clearly, this third man took pride in his sense of accomplishment and his contribution to history. He had the psychological and emotional rush. In addition, he understood that he was far more than just a builder, and he realized that his job was far more important than to just build. His expression of this made other people feel the same way.

### EMOTIONS VERSUS DATA

The first thing the TSR must recognize to become successful is that nobody buys over the telephone solely because of the data they hear from the TSR. Customers buy over the telephone based on emotion. Telephone selling is an emotional industry, and customers react positively when they are emotionally motivated to do so. Why do customers buy books over the telephone? Because they are emotionally motivated to make the purchase. Why do customers change phone service, banking, health plans, insurance companies? Because it feels like the right thing to do. Selling emotions means the TSR sells feelings, word pictures, dynamic images, creativity, euphoria. It means the customer sees what the TSR is selling. The TSR takes those emotions that appeal to the customer and applies them to his product.

As an example, just look at the local baseball field. Hitting a homerun requires the swing of the bat. From the fans' perspective, is that the most exciting thing about the homerun? No. The most exciting thing is seeing the ball go over the fence! The most exciting thing is the rush of the crowds, the music blaring, the scoreboard shouting, the stadium rocking. For the fans, excitement is seeing a homerun clear the fence, because now that fan's team is a run ahead.

Now, let's take a look at the batter's perspective. For the batter, the most exciting thing about a homerun is thrusting his hands in the air, pumping his fists, and circling the bases. The least exciting thing for a batter was swinging the bat. The emotion of winning, the thrill of the crowd, the rush of his teammates all makes a homerun hitter excited, not because he swung the bat, but because he hit the ball. Hitting a homerun is emotional for everybody involved with the game.

Emotion sells everywhere, and telephone selling plays by this rule. Is anybody at the baseball game truly excited because the scoreboard changed? Absolutely not. Scoreboard is data, and scoreboard / data is BORING. It is a mechanical function. The question to ask has nothing to do with the scoreboard. The question to ask is "Why is everybody cheering?"

Because of emotions. And emotions are why customers buy.

Yet, nine out of ten customers would tell you that this isn't true, that instead, they make their decisions logically. If you were in a store and asked ten customers why they had just made a purchase, they would all claim logic and data before emotions. And they would stand by their stories. An example of this arose out of the Kennedy / Nixon election. Logically we know that John F. Kennedy defeated Richard Nixon by less than one percentage point in the 1960 presidential election. Emotionally, after the election was over, more than 75% of voters said they had chosen Kennedy! If I were selling one hundred Kennedy pins to logical voters, I would sell just fifty -one pins. But if I sold one hundred Kennedy pins to emotional voters, I would sell at least seventy five !

Emotions are what sell. Customers mask their emotions because they want to believe that every decision they make is a logical one. The fact is, however, that deep down inside, customers must "want" before they will buy, and this "want" is an emotional reaction. They must "want" to hit a homerun, or win the game, or to have voted for the winner of the election. Making decisions is completely an emotional science. Emotions always reign, and while there may be elements of data involved in the sale, data must always be used in a secondary role. TSRs must recognize that customers buy based on emotions. TSRs must sell emotions!

## DATA SUPPORTS EMOTIONS

There is another reason why emotions are sold successfully over the telephone. It is much easier to sell emotions and then support those emotions with data than it is to sell data and support that data with emotions.

> "Mr. Smith, you are going to have so much <u>fun</u> with this program. And, you are getting this program for the <u>lowest price</u> on the market."

> "Clearly, the exercise gym you're joining will do <u>wonders</u> for not only your children's health, but your parents' health, too. And, because it is located just five minutes from your house, it will be very <u>accessible</u>."

In the match-up of emotions and data, emotions become the dominating venue of choice, but data is the support mechanism that makes emotions credible. I used the example of the baseball homerun and the scoreboard before, and that perfectly illustrates my point. If a fan looked at the scoreboard at the same moment his team had a run added, there would be very little excitement, because there is no emotion to support the data that a run had been added. Then, if a homerun was hit, the emotion for the fan would be less intense, because the fact that the number was added first on the scoreboard took the excitement away. (Why watch a boxing match when you know the winner, and you know the round in which the loser gets knocked down? Why get excited about a touchdown run if you know that data demonstrates your team is going to lose, anyhow? Where is the excitement?) Customers simply do not get excited when they know data first, and then are encouraged to get emotionally worked up because of the data.

Customers do get excited, however, when emotions exist and data supports those emotions. <u>This is a basic principle of telephone selling</u>. The telephone sales representative has the obligation to bring his customer over to his side by emotionally involving him in the conversation and the sell. (When the boss offers somebody a raise, that person is ecstatic. After he offers him the raise, the boss tells that person the additional duties of his job. When a basketball team performs a slam-dunk, the fan is emotionally enthused. Afterward, the fan analyzes the scoreboard and figures out what else is needed to win. When a sales person offers somebody a brand new car, that person is excited about the possibilities. Afterward, he decides whether the data regarding price fits into his price range.)

By selling emotions, the TSR is placing his customer in a mental frame of mind to <u>expect</u>, and expectation sells. Then, when the TSR sells data in order to back up the emotions, the customer understands. By selling data, the TSR delivers. When the data is solid and supportive of emotions, the data will only lend credibility to the project, and help in the telephone sell.

The telephone sales representative has the obligation to bring his customer over to his side by emotionally involving him in the conversation and sell.

Below are eight ways to sell emotions over the telephone, and place the customer in an emotional state of mind.

### 1. Discover What Emotionally Excites the Customer

That which emotionally excites the TSR doesn't necessarily emotionally excite the customer.

"When it comes to buying books, what types of books are irresistible to you?"

### 2. Understand the Customer's Background

Past memories, both good and bad, help to trigger emotions that will create a path so the TSR can sell his product. For example, by asking the question "Do you remember your children's books as a child?" the TSR urges customers to relate their emotional happiness with their books as children to their children's emotional happiness.

### 3. Prepare the Customer for Something Big

Don't make the telephone call an everyday event. Separate the call from other calls.

"I know you get calls all of the time, but believe me when I say that this call is different."

### 4. Help the Customer to Feel Excitement and Enthusiasm

Customers respond to description. On the radio, sports announcers don't say "A swing...and a homerun." Sports announcers say "A swing...and a long drive hit to deep centerfield...back goes the centerfielder...he's at the track...at the wall...looking up...he leaps.......HOMERUN!!!!!"

### 5. Shift Tone, Inflection and Melody

Customers respond to voice patterns. They need to be motivated to move, and that motivation comes from the TSR's shift, at appropriate times.

### 6. Tie the TSR's Emotions into the Customer's Emotions

An inseparable bond between TSRs and customers will make both of them "want".

"We both should be extremely excited about this offer, for a lot of reasons."

### 7. Sell Emotions First

Give customers what they truly want and what they truly need. Have fun.

> "By purchasing these books, your child is going to
> experience a whole new world."

### 8. Utilize Emotional Feel Words

Emotional feel words do make the difference. These words include:

Commitment

Comfort

Pleasure

Benefits

Advantages

Dynamite

Now

See

## WHAT MAKES CUSTOMERS BUY OVER THE TELEPHONE

TSRs are oftentimes confused. They believe, and it is a common mistake, that every valid reason a TSR gives to the customer to make a purchase will appeal emotionally to that customer. Unfortunately, this just isn't true. In fact, I believe that there are only five *real* emotional reasons that customers buy over the telephone. When the TSR focuses on these five reasons to buy, customers tend to respond to one or all of them. When TSRs find other emotional reasons for customers to buy over the telephone, customers become less likely to do so. Below are the five emotional reasons that make customers buy over the telephone:

**TELE-TIP**

There are only five real emotional reasons that make customers buy over the telephone.

### 1. Possession

Customers make buying decisions to become owners. It is very little fun for the customer to make a purchase if he isn't going to be able to have that purchase.

### 2. Prominence

Items become emotionally appealing when they separate one person from another. For example, customers buy beautiful rings, kitchen equipment and clothes because they feel "special" and prominent when they wear or use them. The sales presentation must make the customer stand out.

### 3. Peer Pressure

I have a saying I consistently encourage the telephone sales reps to use when selling to a business. "Mr. Customer, if you have this product and your competition doesn't, you are winning. If your competition has this product and you don't, you are losing. And if you both have this product, then it is the person who uses the product best that will win." Customers say "yes" when they feel that saying "no" may set them back.

### 4. Personal Improvement

I have yet to see a customer make a purchase so he can regress and go backwards. No matter what is sold over the telephone, the TSR needs to paint that product as something that will provide improvement to the customer and to those around him.

### 5. Family

Most customers are sparked to agree to a product when they see how the product benefits their family. For example, if I were selling a music system to a customer who doesn't listen to music, the whole sales presentation would be to emotionally tie that customer's family into the decision making process.

---

**THE CHILDREN'S BOOKS SELLING EXAMPLE**

*When selling children's books, the goal is to get the mother, father, or grandparent emotionally involved in the purchase of the books, for the sake of their children or grandchildren. Then, after they are emotionally involved, the TSR must back up those emotions with positive data. The objective is not to start the presentation by selling the price of the books, or the authors, or even the specific educational value of each book. This comes later. The goal is to get the customer excited.*

"Ms _____, haven't you found, or don't you remember, how valuable good children's books are to young children? The excitement of a good, well developed story. The thrill of meeting new action figures. The pleasure of creatively reading stories about people and worlds and opportunity!!!!!!"

---

## "FEEL" WORDS VERSUS "THINK" WORDS

As the TSR phrases his sentences to keep his customer emotionally involved, he must begin by using special words that spark feelings and de-emphasize thinking words that open up the thought aspect of the purchase. The TSR should be focused on always emphasizing the word "feel" by utilizing variations of the word "feel" in his presentation. What we say is important, and the use of a word like "feel" instead of a word such as "think" makes all the difference in the world when it comes to selling a product.

For example, when the TSR describes something, it is important that he does not say "I think." Instead, he should say "I feel". By stressing the feel portion of his mind, the TSR is making a bolder statement to his customer about what he should do. The way somebody feels makes much more of an impact than what he thinks.

| GOOD | BAD |
|---|---|
| "I feel you should be optimistic" | "I think you should be optimistic" |
| "We want you to feel satisfied" | "We think you should be satisfied" |
| "Many of our other customers feel excited" | "Many of our customers think they should be excited." |
| "Won't you feel curious" | "I think you should be curious" |
| "We feel loyalty" | "I think we have loyalty" |

If the TSR were to sell the way he "thinks" as opposed to the way he "feels", the TSR would be selling indecision as opposed to decisiveness. Something a salesperson "thinks" can be proven otherwise by a customer, because customers know what a salesperson thinks already, and they don't much care. (The salesperson wants the sale) So, when the TSR says "I think", the customer very often begins to believe that the TSR is out for himself.

**TELE-TIP**

A product is only as exciting to a customer as the TSR makes it, and the TSR must do all he can to encourage the customer to feel excited over the product even when the TSR does not find it exciting.

On the other hand, what a sales person "feels" is a whole new ballgame, because what customer can differ with how somebody "feels" about something? Feeling something is much more personal and definitive an emotion, and it is personal and definitive enough to drive the sales process forward!

### FEEL WORDS

Optimistic

Pleased

Relieved

Satisfied

Surprised

Sympathetic

Excited

Elated

Delighted

Curious

Confident

Glad

Happy

Inquisitive

Loyal

Motivated

Wonderful

Outstanding

Dynamic

In addition, the TSR can utilize words in his presentation that allow the customer to see and become motivated. I break these down into two sub-sets: "Compare Words" and "Best Words".

Compare Words involve using words that end with "er". They allow the TSR to frame the debate in a compare / contrast mode, and help the customer picture certain points the TSR is trying to get across about his product. These "er" words include

Faster
"Our product is faster than others."

Better
"Our children's books are better than others."

Bigger
"Our product is bigger than others."

Smarter
"Children become smarter with our product."

Best words take the same tack, but they end with "est". They are selling words that motivate the customer to understand what is the best about a product! These are more absolute words. These "est" words include

Fastest
"Our product is fastest."

Best
"Our children's books are known to be the best."

Biggest
"The biggest product on the market is ours."

Smartest
"We have developed the smartest books for children."

## *"HOW"* IS MORE VALUABLE THAN *"WHAT"*

I teach regularly that *how* a TSR sells throughout a presentation is intrinsically more valuable than *what* is actually said in the presentation. Remember, we have touched upon the fact that customers hear emotions and thrive upon "feel" words, and they don't respond as well to data or "think" words. With this in mind, the *how* of telephone selling correlates to emotions and feel words; the *what* correlates to data and think words. How the TSR portrays himself will affect the number of sales he closes.

Below are three questions to help measure the way in which the TSR portrays himself.

1. **Does the TSR display strong confidence in himself, his product, and his customer?**

   Customers sense when TSRs lack confidence, and this lack of confidence affects three dominating things: the TSR, his product, and his customer.

2. **Does the TSR describe the program with enthusiasm and emotion?**

   The preparation leading up to the presentation should bring about a focus, tone, style and passion that emphasize enthusiasm and emotions.

3. **Does the TSR motivate the customer to act decisively?**

   By selling emotions and feelings, the TSR will motivate the customer. The "How" summarizes who the TSR is, what the sales call is about, and the relationship that will exist between TSR and customer.

When learning why the *how* in telephone selling is important, the TSR must think fundamentals. In baseball, *what* the second baseman does with the baseball after he fields the ball is important. But *how* did the second baseman successfully field the ball? In politics, *what* the politician running for President of the United States does in office is important, but *how* did the candidate for President of the United States earn the right to hold that office? In sales, *what* the TSR says is important, but *how* the TSR expresses himself will encourage the customer to complete the sale.

The *how* and *what* are very difficult techniques to teach, because the science is so imprecise. Some TSRs have a natural knack for selling the *how* portion of a presentation far more easily than selling the *what* portion of a presentation. The *how* portion involves panache, style, creativity, spontaneity, levity, depth. The *what* portion of a presentation involves study, research, practice, knowledge, intellect. To sum up the *how* versus the *what*, always remember this: *how* the TSR communicates over the telephone is far more important than *what* he communicates . And much of *how* the TSR communicates stems from comprehending themes, images and concepts.

## THEMES, IMAGES AND CONCEPTS

Selling emotions and feelings. How exciting!!! If only selling emotions were so simple. If only it were easy for a telephone sales rep to get on the phone and complete sale after sale because he and his customers are immersed in the emotional element of the sales call. This doesn't happen very often, and in some instances, it is not because of a lack of effort on the TSR's side. In some instances, the product a TSR is selling over the telephone, no matter how emotional he tries to make it sound, is a very unemotional product. For example, children's books can be emotional. Oil filters can be unemotional. Donating blood for charity can be emotional. Changing long distance phone service can be unemotional.

**TELE-TIP**

By stressing the feel portion of his mind, the TSR is making a bolder statement to his customer about what he should do.

How, then, can a TSR who practices the principles of selling emotions before data successfully sell an unemotional product? In order to do so, two prerequisites must be in place.

The TSR must have thorough knowledge of his product
The TSR must be extremely creative

Assuming these prerequisites exist, the TSR must then implement the process I call themes, images and concepts. Themes, images and concepts are real sales tools used to complete sales over the telephone. They are the tools that provide to customers pictures that help them understand what is being sold. In essence, just because a product the TSR is selling is boring doesn't mean the customer will consider it boring. Just because the TSR is not turned on by oil filters or phone service doesn't mean that the customer won't be. A product is only as exciting to a customer as the TSR makes it, and the TSR must do all he can to encourage the customer to feel excited over the product even when the TSR does not find it exciting. This is done by selling themes, images and concepts of the product so that the customer can see them come to life. When customers get excited about a product, they are telling the telephone sales representative what will and will not work.

I have placed themes, images and concepts in the Understanding Telephone Selling chapter because they comprise elements of telephone selling that most TSRs never really learn. They tie in directly with the objective of selling emotions and feel words to the customer, because themes, images and concepts represent imagery and metaphors.

Themes, images and concepts go to the creative heart of a telephone sales representative's job. It is nearly impossible for a telephone sales rep to sell themes, images and concepts while not being creative. This leads me to the crux of the way I teach. I can't emphasize enough how important it is for the TSR to think creatively on the telephone. Why? Because it's a given on each call that the customer will be less creative with regard to the product than is the TSR, and a sale will be that much more difficult to complete if the TSR settles for creativity equal to the customer's.

Let's explore this a step further. Remember in the previous chapter when we touched upon visuals and verbals? If I were to ask ten TSRs what sub-venue they utilize to sell, they would say they sell verbals, and they would be correct. We have already explored the fact that telephone selling is predominately a verbal medium. But what all ten TSRs won't tell you is that they also sell visuals over the phone!!! Visuals are creative descriptions of the product, so the customer is taught how to visually "see" while communicating with the telephone sales rep. This is the imagery, the picture framing, and the general thrust of selling themes, images and concepts. So customers can see.

Selling themes, images and concepts relies on what I call visual demonstration. The job of a creative TSR is to visually demonstrate to the customer exactly how the product is perfect for him. And the way to do that is to involve the customer in the emotional excitement of themes, images and concepts of the product.

Anybody who has performed telephone selling recognizes that the one constant all TSRs battle is indecision with regard to how to communicate information clearly and persuasively *and* in a way that motivates the customer to respond. Themes, images and concepts comprise a theory of telephone selling that I have developed that relates to communicating messages. It is my belief that customers on the receiving end of a telephone presentation hear very little when it comes to the actual words that are spoken. Instead, they respond very strongly to the messages that are spoken, and these messages are conveyed, from the TSR to the customer, through the channel of images, concepts and themes.

## BACKGROUND

Have you ever had a phone conversation with a friend? We all have, and we all have phone conversations every day. The question then becomes "How many exact words does one remember from a conversation?" The answer of course is none, because people don't take away words from a conversation. They take away the themes, images and concepts that one person is trying to get across to another. In any form of sales, themes, images and concepts are what move products. In telephone selling, nobody says "yes" to a product offer because of words. Instead, it's the motivation of what can be, presented by the TSR in a way that transcends phrases, which sells the product. With in-person selling, this can be demonstrated by showing examples; a wave of the hand, the eye making contact. Words complement these actions. Over the phone, however, it is the painting of themes, images and concepts that brings customers to the next level. Therefore, the words that are spoken are not nearly as important to a telephone call as the way those words demonstrate the vision. As I mentioned before, the way the TSR coordinates visual demonstration is extremely important to the success of a telephone sales call.

To provide an example, take the comparison of radio commercials and telephone selling, which are two similar mediums, because they both reach people and attempt to move products based on voice. Those who produce radio commercials are far ahead of those who provide TSR training, because those who write radio commercials have found that it is the idea of themes, images and concepts that moves products. When studying recent radio commercials, we learned that in the Carl's Junior campaign, no one listening will remember anything that is said in the commercial except for *"If it doesn't get all over the place, it doesn't belong in your face"*. This line provides the listener with a theme, an image and a concept about Carl's Junior's hamburgers that supersedes all of the other words that are spoken.

## FIVE ACTIONS TO TEACH TSRs HOW TO
## SELL THEMES, IMAGES AND CONCEPTS

### 1. Move TSRs away from the "words thing"

The "words thing" bothers TSRs to no end. Many TSRs spend hundreds of hours trying to perfect the perfect words that they can use over the phone. They try to articulate every word as if each word can make the sale, when all they need to do is to learn the product that they are selling like the back of their hand, and focus their work effort on creating new and exciting visual demonstrations for the customer. Most TSRs who try to find those perfect phrases over the telephone are really substituting their effort to develop perfect phrases with their inability to understand the concept of their product in a creative fashion. Those TSRs who understand their product creatively worry very little about what to say, because they spend all of their time studying how to say it. Your job as sales manager is to first provide thorough training to your TSRs on all facets of the product, and then teach your TSRs the images, themes and concepts that can be visually associated with your product.

### 2. Teach TSRs analogies that can visually demonstrate the product

I have found that the best way to sell over the telephone is to incorporate the themes, images and concepts of your product into analogies that the customer can clearly comprehend. Customers are motivated to buy a product only when they completely understand the purchase, and analogies lend credibility by opening up visual pathways. Analogies also allow the TSR to create present everyday situations that customers encounter and tie them into the product. For example, if a customer is unsure whether it is best to buy more computer hard drives for his business, analogize the decision with buying new tennis shoes for his children. Analogies such as this are simple, easy to follow, and do more for selling a product than almost anything else. "Mr._____, do you have children? How many? When do they usually get new clothes? What new clothes do they like to get most? How important is it that they get new shoes? Mr._____, your decision on whether to buy new computer hard drives is exactly the same as your decision regarding buying new clothes and shoes for your children. How many computers do you have? How many hard drives do you need? When have you purchased new computer equipment before? How important is it to the company that they get these new hard drives?" Many TSRs fail to realize how important creativity can be, and selling analogies can open up a new comfort level of selling between the TSR and customers.

### 3. Choose four benefits of the product that can best represent the product's images

How many millions of times have we heard that selling over the telephone involves selling benefits? What we haven't heard is that selling benefits involves selling images. Benefits are nothing more than images of a product. Hence, if your product is children's books, the benefits to the reader can be many, (educational, long lasting, inexpensive). The image the TSR must present, however, will either make or break the selling of the benefits. Is the image of these benefits an image that promotes healthy readership? Does the image of these benefits make the customer understand the genuine quality and craftsmanship that go into each book? Does the image of these benefits communicate to the customer that the books will provide a sense of value to the child? As a sales manager, you must train your TSRs to understand the images that should be associated with the benefits. Unfortunately, far too often, benefits are communicated quickly and simply, and images are never accurately conveyed to the customer.

4. **Develop three transition lines that will introduce the theme of each benefit**

   How many times has a customer heard a TSR talk about a benefit while the customer had absolutely no idea what was going on in the conversation? There is a simple way to teach TSRs how to prevent this error. Transition lines are the hidden element to a dynamic telephone sales call. Prior to the communication of benefits, there needs to be an introduction to the benefits. These transition lines present the theme of what the TSR wishes to communicate, and they usually come in the form of a question. For example, prior to communicating a benefit and image of children's books, the TSR can say "Ms._____, is it really tough trying to find some good books for your children now-a-days? What action-adventure stories really interest your children?" By beginning with these transition lines, the customer is able to visually understand the process of the telephone call. First, interest the customer in a certain type of children's book. Then sell the benefits of that type of children's book. If the benefits part of a presentation is the image the TSR is trying to project, then the transition lines to promote the benefits are the themes the TSR must visually demonstrate.

5. **Select Three features for each benefit that provide the concept of the product.**

   I believe the only way to successfully sell benefits is to also sell the features that support each benefit. Many times we teach TSRs how to sell benefits without realizing that selling benefits is not enough. Features provide credibility to those benefits and, without features, the customer would have great difficulty learning the concept of the product being sold. For example, if a benefit to children's books is that the books are educational, a feature would be that the books were written by some of the best educators in the country. If a benefit is that each book has large, glossy illustrated pictures, then the feature would be that there are no less than eight large, glossy illustrated pictures in every book, produced by the greatest artists of the 20th century. Features emphasize concept, and concept visually demonstrates to the customer exactly why he should be motivated to do something.

## STRENGTHS AND REPETITION

The best part of a TSR's job is to relax in a soft and comfortable chair with a favorite drink. If I took a poll of what the best perks to a telephone sales job are, the laziness of activity combined with the accessibility of food and snack will always be in the top ten. I am a big believer that TSRs should enjoy the luxury of food and drink at their desks, at all times. This always leads me into a battle with other managers, because protecting the cost of computer and phone equipment always seems to outweigh the encouragement of production. Little do most people realize that it is the incentive of allowing food and drink at a desk that not only increases production in the short term, but maximizes production and stability in the long term. The job of telephone selling is so mentally grinding that it is important that all the "little things" such as food and beverage, are very accessible to each TSR.

I remember that, as a manager in one evening job, I had difficulty impacting the Friday night shift. Although our account would be full Monday through Thursday, we would only have 40% attendance on Friday. What is a manager to do in Los Angeles? Instead of forcing and coercing TSRs to come to work, which is a philosophy I long considered, I took a different approach. If you can't beat them, join them. Hence, I developed "Free Food Fridays", which turned Fridays into our most popular shift of the week. Instead of having my TSRs miss work to go to a Friday night party, I had the Friday night party come to work. Every Friday, I purchased an assortment of food and beverages, and stashed them in the break room. I eliminated periodic breaks, instead allowing each TSR to come and go from the break room to their desk as they pleased. In addition, I increased the amount of games and contests we played that day while adding music to the ambiance of the sales floor. It was a controlled yet fun and wild evening for everybody!!!! Although production suffered slightly in relation to the other four days of the week, production greatly *increased* in relation to our previous Friday numbers. In fact, we more than doubled our Friday output, while falling just points shy of beating our production throughout the week.

The point of this story is simple. As a manager, flexibility is foremost in motivating and leading TSRs. But more importantly, as a TSR it is clear that playing to one's strengths through repetition is the only way to succeed when selling over the telephone. Playing to strengths through repetition is as much a contributing factor in creating a dynamic telephone presentation than anything else. To increase my Friday sales production I had to play to the strengths of my environment, and that involved loosening the shirt and bringing a Friday night party to my Los Angeles call center. Every Friday. Consistently. As a TSR, your strengths through repetition are just as important. This is why TSRs all throughout America are much more like world champion weight lifters than they could ever imagine.

Let's look at the parallel. Weightlifting is a brute sport, based on practice, desire, focus, and of course, strength through repetition. Weightlifters of all shapes and sizes in all classes spend hours each day refining their skills in

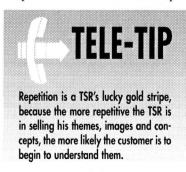

**TELE-TIP**

Repetition is a TSR's lucky gold stripe, because the more repetitive the TSR is in selling his themes, images and concepts, the more likely the customer is to begin to understand them.

front of the weights for that one moment, perhaps two, when they can demonstrate their talents and become the best in the world. It is a physical test of endurance, but it is also a mental test of endurance, and I think it is important to recognize that very few people are aware of the mental part. Lifting weights involves the mind, and any weightlifter will tell you that!!! Most importantly, weightlifting, both from a physical and mental perspective, involves strength through repetition. That brings me to how I see a tremendous parallel between weightlifters and TSRs. Sure, weightlifters pick up hundreds of pounds worth of weights, while TSRs pick up a telephone and / or a coffee mug. Sure, weightlifters are almost always silent, until they pick up the weights, when they let out a GRRRRUNT that would terrorize the best of us. TSRs are never silent – they are talking, selling, communicating machines.

So where is the parallel? The parallel exists in the strength through repetition. Just like weightlifting, telephone selling is a sport made up of practice, desire, focus, and of course, strength through repetition. Weightlifting may be a brute sport while telephone selling is a finesse sport, but the parallel exists because both are mental sports.

Within the spectrum of a telephone call, TSRs are asked to sell one aspect of their program: the strengths. And in order to sell that one aspect of the program, the TSR must accentuate, over and over again, every single strength of the program, through repetition. We touched upon how customers don't listen to the words TSRs use; they remember the themes, images and concepts. Hence, repetition is a TSR's lucky gold stripe, because the more repetitive the TSR is in selling his themes, images and concepts, the more likely the customer is to begin to understand them.

I teach in sales training courses that 90% of all customers don't remember anything that is said in a telephone sales call with the exception of the themes, images and concepts of the call. This is an amazing fact, and it is one that many telephone sales trainers don't explore in enough depth and detail.

If you take it at its face value, all of those words that are spoken, all of the interaction, statements, questions, responses and buzz words between customer and TSR really amount to nothing short of a hill of beans – 90% is forgotten, just 10% is retained. By using repetition as an advantage, the TSR can frame the telephone presentation so as to direct it to where he wants it to go.

For example, if the TSR wants to emphasize the point that the customer must like children's books because of the beautiful color illustrations, it is necessary for the TSR to sell those beautiful color illustrations a minimum of five times throughout the conversation. It is my belief that if the TSR sells color illustrations less than five times, the customer won't completely understand their true value, and hence the strengths of the sell won't be communicated effectively.

Telephone selling is all about repetition. To give a personal example, in my telephone sales training courses I communicate to my class before the course begins that I tend to repeat myself throughout the seminar, to the point where the TSRs can recite what I am about to say, over and over and over again. I inform them that I don't do this because I forget easily or because I think they are too slow to understand what I am teaching, but instead, because I understand that about 80% of what I will say gets lost, and only 20% is even understood, in a classroom setting. It is that 20%, the important 20%, that I consistently repeat over and over and over again so each TSR understands it. TSRs must utilize this example of the strength of repetition in their sales presentations to customers if they hope to close sales over the telephone.

As TSRs continue to understand telephone selling and their role in it, society will become accustomed to accepting telephone selling. We began this chapter with a study of how emotions overcome data when persuading on the telephone, and how data actually becomes a support vehicle when selling emotions. In addition, we reviewed those things that encourage customers to buy, such as feel words, and *how* we communicate as opposed to *what* we communicate. Finally, we concluded this chapter by studying themes, images and concepts, and how strengths and repetition make sales. This chapter is truly a set-up chapter for the one that follows, when we take everything we learned here and apply it to the one thing that will eventually encourage society to accept telephone selling: establishing credibility.

# CHAPTER  3

## SELLING CREDIBILITY

Successfully selling over the telephone can be terribly frustrating when one imagines what could happen to a telephone call <u>if the TSR doesn't take the initiative of establishing some form of credibility extremely early in the conversation.</u> Without establishing credibility, the TSR becomes a monster to the customer, due to the customer's fear and lack of confidence in the TSR. Even the most viable customer becomes most difficult when the TSR fails to establish credibility. The frustration of selling over the telephone is three-fold due to the fact that no matter how well a TSR does everything else in a telephone sales presentation, the inability to create credibility will sink the whole ship. In telephone sales, the way the customer *perceives* the TSR makes all of the difference between completing a sale or missing a sale. In this book we explore the fact that the customer can't see the TSR, and depending on the circumstances, that could be very positive or very negative. If the customer requires intimacy before agreeing to a sale, a lack of personal contact (i.e. seeing one another) could very well endanger the completion of the sale. If the TSR can establish credibility early, however, he may be able to make customer needs an inconsequential factor to the sale. In this book we also explore the fact that history has taught customers of today to be very wary of TSRs, and telephone sales presentations in general. What was once a credible forum for selling fifty years ago began to lose its luster about twenty years ago when the unsavory "make-a-buck-quick" companies began to form. Because there are so many good, solid companies performing telephone selling correctly, the image is slowly on the rebound. (With help from the information age of computers, the Internet, cable television and home shopping networks.)

With this in mind, the frustration for a TSR comes when the TSR knows he is honest, knows his product is good, and knows the customer likes what he hears, but still **can't** earn the trust and confidence and credibility of the customer!! Perhaps it's because this particular customer needs visuals instead of verbals. Or perhaps, history and society have taught this particular customer not to trust TSRs and telephone sales calls. In any event, it is the TSR's job to find out, and establish some form of credibility early in order to thwart these problems.

When I speak of establishing credibility, I speak of establishing credibility *with the customer*, so the customer feels comfortable, at ease and confident about the telephone conversation. The TSR must resolve four points throughout a conversation in order to establish credibility with the customer:

1. **The TSR must establish himself as a credible entity...**

   Customers do not make decisions over the telephone if they don't feel the TSR is completely credible, all of the time. The TSR must be a friend and a partner.

2. **The TSR must establish his telephone call as a credible process...**

   Customers have learned to be wary of telephone solicitations, so the TSR must portray his call as something different from all the other run-of-the-mill phone calls.

3. **The TSR must establish his product / client as credible...**

   Customers make decisions over the telephone only when they feel that what they are getting will benefit them. TSRs must establish their products / clients as truly exceptional .

4. **The TSR must implement the decision-making process as a credible process ...**

   Saying "yes" and completing a sale over the telephone is the customer's most agonizing decision. Any doubt on the customer's part will eliminate his ability to say "yes".

I am a firm believer that credibility is the most tricky proposition TSRs will encounter. I like to think back to the political career of former president Richard Nixon to put into perspective why credibility is such a tricky proposition. Throughout his political career, Nixon struggled to establish himself as a credible force. Although he had suc-

**TELE-TIP**

Without establishing credibility, the TSR becomes a monster to the customer, due to the customer's fear and lack of confidence in the TSR.

cesses and failures when both running for political office and while serving, Nixon never truly was able to establish himself as a credible figure in the public eye. From 1953-1961, he was Dwight Eisenhower's vice president, but he was never looked at as a credible figure who might one day successfully command the presidency. When running for president in 1960 against John Kennedy, Kennedy was able to generate far more acceptability than Nixon for many reasons, all of which had a part in Nixon shyly losing the election. Moving forward, when Nixon was president from 1969-1974, many citizens couldn't feel comfortable with Nixon, his views, and his personality.

Credibility extends to trust, as we will see later in this chapter, and in many ways Nixon was unable to foster that trust. I see Nixon as a partial success, but I view him as one who was never completely successful, and I feel that has something to do with the fact that he was never able to formulate that element of credibility with his public that is needed for success

Here is another example. I recently received three different telemarketing calls at my house. On the first call, I noted the TSR wasn't even paying attention to what she was doing. I said "hello" three separate times before she responded! By that time, she had lost all credibility. The second caller was fairly efficient, and although I didn't purchase the product, I noted that the TSR did a good job. The third telephone call was from a gentleman who sounded like he was afraid of his own shadow. Just hearing him say his name made me want to cringe, and I picked up from his first sentence that this TSR was going to establish little credibility. I said a quick "not interested", and the TSR said a quicker "Okay, goodbye", and then hung up!

TSRs find establishing credibility a very difficult proposition. Credibility is never a need of the TSR. Instead, credibility is a need that the customer has. In addition, TSRs must remain cognizant of the fact that each customer is an individual completely separate from every other individual. Therefore, the things the TSR must say to make the customer feel the telephone call is credible are quite different for each customer. Discovering what those differences are for each customer goes a long, long way toward creating credibility with that customer at that moment.

Another aspect of telephone selling that continuously hinders TSRs in establishing credibility is the common assumption that they are being received by the customer as credible, when in reality they aren't. For no other reason except that the TSR thinks of himself as very credible, the TSR has a misguided confidence that this total stranger on the telephone is feeling the same way about him! Of course, I preach self-confidence in all of my sales training workshops and throughout this book, and I am a strong believer that *confidence* is a major asset when establishing credibility. However, TSRs forget that each customer is different, and hence, they don't spend enough time in each telephone presentation building up their own credibility. For example, it is safe to say that on many calls the customer is going to be skeptical in some way about what the TSR is saying. This especially happens when a product offer is particularly good, or when the benefits and features being sold are "oversold" by the TSR (a topic which we will explore later). A common statement I have heard a million times from customers is "This all sounds too good to be true". This is a statement, not a question. In a question format, the customer is asking the TSR to disprove his theory that "Doesn't this all sound too good to be true?" Questions are good, because questions mean the customer believes in the credibility of the TSR and also wants the TSR to inform him. Whenever questions are asked, then the customer is interested. But when customers make the statement "This all sounds too good to be true", they are saying they don't believe what they are hearing, and don't have enough confidence in the TSR to ask him to inform them. By making this statement, the customer is letting the TSR know that he isn't open enough at this stage to allow the TSR to tell him exactly why it isn't too good to be true. When making statements, the customer is saying "Now Mr. TSR, don't tug at my chain and take me for a ride." When making statements, the customer is not asking "How can I believe you?" Motivating the customer to ask "How can I believe you?" is what all TSRs must aim for when establishing credibility.

This leads me to a story from the late 1980's. As a sports radio announcer in the minor leagues, I once spent a season providing play-by-play for a minor league basketball team. We had a player on our team who was truly outstanding. (For the purposes of this story, we'll name him Mike McClosky.) He could shoot from the outside, handle the basketball fairly well, was a quality citizen, and constantly commanded the respect and confidence of his peers around our league. But he couldn't break into the NBA. One day, I sat down and interviewed this player for my pre-game show, which preceded the start of each game. I asked him point blank "Will you ever play in the NBA?" With outstanding confidence and a solid smile, he replied "Definitely. I definitely will play in the NBA. I have all the tools to make it there, and I will make it. I just haven't received my chance." More than eight years later, this player still hasn't reached the NBA, and won't, because he failed at two things that impact credibility. First, he didn't establish credibility with the coaches and general managers around the NBA. Second, he never truly recognized what he needed to do to become credible.

Although the coaches and general managers around our minor league felt that Mike McClosky was a great player, the coaches and general managers in the NBA could see distinctly that he lacked quickness for a shooting guard, and the defensive skills necessary to guard either the point guard, shooting guard or small forward in an NBA setting. Every comment from NBA coaches and general managers to Mike McClosky was the same: "If you improve on your defense and add some quickness, we'll take a look at you." But Mike McClosky insisted on focusing on his strengths rather than attempting to resolve his weaknesses. Instead of working on the skills which would make him credible to the NBA (quickness and defense), he focused on scoring, passing and dribbling, which were three traits he didn't need to accentuate.

Hence, as every year went by he continued to lose credibility with the NBA coaches and general managers. And because he never identified and resolved the things he needed to do to establish credibility, he never made it to the NBA.

## THREE CIRCUMSTANCES WHICH CAN IMPACT CREDIBILITY

There are three things that have the potential to greatly impact the credibility of a telephone sales presentation:

The TSR

The customer

The product

I am a firm believer that finding a wonderful company that employs good TSRs, and provides good customers and a good product is extremely challenging. Many companies may fulfill two of the three categories, and some companies might have variations of the three categories, but very few companies provide the TSRs, customer base and product that all come together to form an outstanding offer.

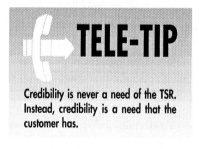

**TELE-TIP**

Credibility is never a need of the TSR. Instead, credibility is a need that the customer has.

Of these three circumstances, the TSR is completely responsible only for himself, while he has the job duty of doing the best he can to make an <u>impact on controlling</u> the customer and the product. If all three of these circumstances are favorable, there is an excellent chance that a sale will be completed. What a TSR hopes for on every call is that he is in a wonderful rhythm, that the customer is capable of being placed in a wonderful rhythm, and that the product is capable of being presented well by the TSR to a customer <u>who needs it</u>. On the other hand, if the TSR is not on his game, the customer and product can do little to bail him out. The TSR is the central communications point, and analogous to a point guard on the basketball court, the TSR must be on his game so he can distribute information appropriately.

If the customer absolutely refuses to hear a presentation, the TSR's role becomes much less important. No matter how talented the TSR is, <u>the customer must be a willing player in the communications game</u>. If the product doesn't have appeal to the customer at the point of presentation, the customer isn't going to budge. The TSR may be viewed as an offensive point guard, and the customer as the defensive team. In this case, the product is the sport being played. That sport needs to draw people. It needs to be entertaining, exciting, worth taking a look at. Without a good product, like a good sport, the players participating would be rendered meaningless.

Of these three entities, it is the product that most greatly impacts a telephone sales presentation. The product being sold always affects the final determination of how well the TSR, customer and product will work together. Products can affect the type of people hired to represent them, the type of people who are being called to possibly purchase them, and of course the products themselves. Therefore, while the TSR must understand exactly what is needed to establish credibility with the customer, it is important to recognize that the true success or failure of a telephone sales project was decided long before the first TSR was hired; by the company responsible for the product.

## THE TSR

The TSR is the first entity to establish credibility with the customer. This is most easily accomplished when the TSR is prepared, prior to the telephone presentation, to sell in every way possible. <u>It is safe to say that there is nothing like an unprepared TSR to provoke doubt in the mind of a customer.</u> As an example, I recently went to a restaurant that had no menu or wine list. When we asked what kind of wine was in stock, the waiter responded with "I really don't know. I'm not sure." This didn't allow me to have the most confidence in my waiter – his restaurant was quickly losing credibility with me, and I started to wonder how much this meal, and wine he didn't know about, would cost me! It's not enough for a TSR to realize that he has to be prepared with regard to what he is selling. Preparation takes a lot of time and energy, and it involves truly understanding the product being sold. To prepare for the presentation the TSR must consider the following:

What is the product about?

Who are the competitors?

What are some of the types of questions that might be asked?

How much does the product cost?

Will price be a determining factor for the customer?

How much are the competitors' prices?

What are some of the reasons a customer should
purchase this product?

There are various ways to prepare for a telephone sales project. Most obviously, the company the TSR is working for should have a training program designed to answer the above questions, and many others. In addition, it is absolutely necessary for TSRs to take time away from work to do additional research on their products. In this age of technology, the Internet is quickly supplanting the library as an effective means of quality research. In addition to the Internet and the library, resources such as magazines, newspapers and competitors' programs provide ways to become more knowledgeable about the product and more credible to the customer, prior to the inception of calling.

## THE CUSTOMER

How a customer is going to receive a telephone call is somewhat out of the hands of the TSR. Dialing the telephone and communicating with somebody new can be as pleasurable at one end of the spectrum as old friends talking for the first time in years and as distasteful at the other end as seething enemies who never want to talk again. In a regular list of customer names, the usual conversion percentage of a telephone sales project ranges from 2% to 20%, depending on the three circumstances mentioned above (TSR, Customer, Product). There are so many hidden factors in a telephone sales call that even the best "call lists"

**TELE-TIP**

There is nothing like an unprepared TSR to provoke doubt in the mind of a customer.

can give sales managers an idea of how a telephone sales program will go, but not a definite prediction. For example, I have worked on sales accounts where 5% conversion was good, and others where 15% was average. It all depends. <u>Most relevant, though, are the hidden customer factors that can make or break the credibility of a telephone sales call.</u> Some of those factors follow.

● **When is the TSR calling the customer?**

Some customers only want to be called at a certain time of night and become very poor customers at every other time. Some business people only wish to accept solicitations in the morning hours before a great rush; some in the evening hours.

● **What is happening around the customer when the TSR calls?**

The most jovial customer can turn into a raving lunatic if contacted while he is eating dinner or spending time with his children, or fighting with his significant other. In addition, calling business owners while they are in the height of consumer traffic is the wrong move as well, because they are most concerned with taking care of their customers.

● **Who else has contacted the customer?**

The early bird catches the worm. Perhaps by the time the customer is called, he has already completed a sale with somebody else. Or the customer has received a telephone call from somebody else and wishes to continue the relationship with him.

There are so many variables that affect the customer that the TSR is pretty much incapable of controlling them. <u>The TSR can limit them by trying to work around them when these variables do take place</u>. But luck, timing and good fortune define what the TSR is going to encounter when he calls the customer.

## THE PRODUCT

This area impacts credibility the most. I have yet to see a good TSR sell a poor product on a consistent and successful basis. Certainly, once in a while a good TSR is able to sell a poor product, but in the long run this is no fun for the TSR or the customer. In fact, poor products just hurt the telephone sales industry. Reality dictates that only with a good product can successful selling be accomplished.

In actuality, good products sometimes sell themselves. For example, I was managing a telephone sales project where the product was so valuable for the customers that the mere mention of it sparked considerable interest. This was like stealing candy from a baby or, more appropriately, it was like giving candy to a baby! It was a good product, had a good image, received good customer reaction, and it all amounted to completed sales.

With this in mind, here are five ways that products can establish the credibility needed for completed sales:

1. **The Product Must Appeal To the Customer**

No customer will purchase a product that doesn't offer the customer value in return. If the TSR is selling healthy vegetables to a vegetarian, the TSR has a good product. If the TSR is selling unhealthy vegetables to a vegetarian, the customer may be good but the product isn't.

2. **The Product Must Have A Track Record of Success**

Being involved with the California Labor and Employment Law BI-Monthly, I have a first hand experience to recount. When we tried selling our product in a mass-market approach on day one, we had no clients and no credibility to back up our claims. We scaled back and established a small but consistent subscriber base. With this base, our mass- market approach then worked.

### 3. The Product Must Match, Or Exceed, Its Competition

Good products lose big when they don't maintain competitiveness with the competition. For example, American autos in the 1970's were excellent, but increased technology by the competition in the early 1980's outpaced their efforts. In the late 1980's, even though American autos caught up with and may even have surpassed their competition, they were unable to make a serious dent in the market. Why? Because the product had been non-competitive for too long.

### 4. The Product Must Sell Itself

This is a critical factor. I have debates all of the time with owners and presidents who truly believe that a TSR can sell what doesn't exist. They believe this because telephone selling is a verbal medium. I claim, on the other hand, that good products have enough features to sell themselves, regardless of the skills of the TSRs. In any event, good products must be able to sell themselves without the benefit of a second party.

### 5. The Product Must Be Adaptable

Good products are exactly like good people. Good products provide solid, consistent messages about themselves, but they are <u>flexible</u> when it comes to the sales process. Rigid products produce rigid TSRs who encounter rigid customers. A product that refuses to bend in price, responsibilities, or terms and conditions is a product that can succeed, <u>but limits itself</u>. A good product is one that allows the TSR some room to move through the course of a presentation.

## OVERSELLING THE PROGRAM

Have you ever tried so hard to establish credibility that credibility was lost in the process? I have. Her name was Kimberly, and we were in the ninth and tenth grade. Each day before walking to school, I would try to time when Kimberly would walk past my street. I would leave my house so we could walk together, and during our walk I would do my best to sell her on me. I offered to carry her books. I offered to buy her a newspaper. I even offered to drive her to school when I got my license toward the end of 10th grade. I was crazy about her, and I thought I had to give everything I had to sell myself. One time, I talked her into giving me her phone number, and I asked her out on a date. She responded that she would get back to me, and days went by. Finally, I called her up and talked to her, and as I think back on the incident, it was clear she was stalling because of a lack of interest. After fifteen minutes of selling myself some more and not being able to complete the close, I became frustrated, told her I wasn't going to ask again because she had to say "yes" or "no", and then I abruptly ended the phone call. (Did I hang up on her? I don't think so!)

It was probably the first sale I lost, and at the time it seemed life ending.

Clearly, I oversold, and I learned quickly that overselling the product is one of the fastest ways to lose credibility in a telephone sales call. There is a point when continuing to sell crosses the line from creative TSR to blustery and irritating TSR. There is a point when selling no longer becomes a conversation, but turns into a contest. There is a point when the customer decides the conversation has taken a turn on a road he doesn't appreciate. There is a point when selling the product becomes less and less persuasive to the customer. These points are called <u>overselling</u>, and they are what the TSR must avoid throughout a presentation, because these points, while very subtle, cost many TSRs sales. In training sessions, I preach over and over again that in certain situations it is much better to undersell a program well than to oversell a program terribly. I believe this to be true because by underselling well, the TSR can limit what he is selling and avoid confusing the customer. In addition, by underselling, the TSR is assuring both himself and the customer that if he can't complete the sale that way, he can always continue to sell more, because he has left himself some latitude. In my dating experience, I tried so hard to oversell who I was and what I wanted that I never gave Kimberly the opportunity to be an equal partner in the relationship.

## HOW TO STOP FROM OVERSELLING THE PROGRAM

Below are blueprints for TSRs to study so they can stop themselves from overselling their programs.

*First,* it is critical that the TSR understand the points in a telephone sales presentation when he first begins overselling, and why. Hopefully, the TSR will realize when overselling begins and stay away from there. Yet even if he misses that point and creeps into an oversell, he must understand where he is and back away before losing the customer. When customers start saying things such as "I got that part" or "You mentioned that already" or "I understand, I understand", the TSR should realize the sale is drifting away. This is the customers' way of saying that they don't want to hear something over again, because what they are hearing just flat out doesn't work. Much of overselling begins when the TSR begins selling portions of a product that don't work for the customer. This is very subjective on the customer's part. For example, the TSR may believe he is selling an important point of his program, but the customer may consider that point inconsequential. Thus, the customer perceives the TSR is overselling. As we have discussed in previous

**TELE-TIP**

In training sessions, I preach over and over again that in certain situations it is much better to undersell a program well than to oversell a program terribly.

chapters, <u>TSRs should have a plan of what they want to sell and how they want to sell it</u>. Throughout the telephone call, they work their plan until it is exhausted, or the sale is completed. Once the plan has been worked, there should be little need to go over the plan again. Repeating <u>unnecessarily</u> is a requisite of overselling. (I once had a boss who continually preached "You must plan a plan, plan the plan to work, and work the plan." I took that to mean I should be organized. I learned from him that by planning a plan, planning the plan to work, and working the plan, my TSRs didn't oversell!)

*Second*, the TSR must understand what he is trying to sell to the customer. Many times TSRs oversell a program because they didn't sell the program correctly the first time. This happens quite often with TSRs who are unprepared, but it also happens to TSRs who haven't analyzed the correct areas of the product efficiently enough. In this scenario, TSRs discuss the benefits of a program without truly understanding those benefits themselves, and hence the customer becomes confused. TSRs, thinking they haven't expressed that benefit yet, or well enough, sell it again, only in a different way. Because neither the TSR nor customer truly understands what is going on, the TSR attempts a third stab at it, and now confusion reigns. The TSR is overselling the program by overselling the same benefits.

*Third*, the TSR needs to establish a special relationship with the customer. Those TSRs who haven't effectively developed that special rapport find themselves at a loss when communicating with the customer. I have a real good friend who prides himself on being a good telephone sales representative, and a good sales person in general. Often, we will discuss a topic and he will make his point so well that I will actually say "Okay, I'm with you". You would think that would be enough for him to drop the topic and move on, but it isn't. He will continue to pound home his points over and over again to the point where I have to say "Hey, I'm on your side. You made your points. Don't oversell!" The situation here is that, although we are good friends, we don't have good rapport with one another, and I can't ever figure it out. We communicate, but not fluently. We talk, but it is stilted. The chemistry is missing. More important is the fact that because this rapport is missing, he doesn't understand when he wins and when he loses, so he keeps on going. This is a common error many telephone sales representatives make.

They keep going and going and going even after they have achieved their primary goal. This overselling actually ends up hurting them, because they talk themselves right out of completed sales. Is it because they don't have good listening and hearing skills? Is it because they enjoy selling so much that they would rather oversell than complete a sale? Is it because they like hearing their own voices? Is it because they don't understand their primary goal and secondary objectives? Is it because they can't foster rapport and chemistry? Is it because they aren't quite familiar with the product they are selling? Perhaps all of the above.

*Fourth,* the TSR must always spend time with the customer asking questions, trial closing, and closing. We will explore these telephone sales techniques in greater depth in later chapters, but it is important to recognize that when a customer communicates with the TSR, he tells the TSR everything he needs to know about the sale. In this respect, he tells the TSR when the TSR is beginning to oversell, or if the TSR has undersold. It is the telephone sales representative's responsibility, not the customer's, to ask questions of the customer and make sure he is satisfied with what he has heard at each stage. These questions should be designed to deduce what else, if anything, the TSR needs to say to complete the sale. Obviously, if the customer asks questions of the TSR or delivers quality responses, then it is safe to say that the TSR has not oversold and has probably played it safe by underselling. This is always good, because whenever the customer asks questions it means the TSR has sparked interest. When attempting to establish credibility, what a TSR wants more than anything else is for the customer to start asking the TSR questions. If the customer has no questions of the TSR, then it might mean that the product has been sold to its maximum capacity.

## ELICITING QUESTIONS FROM THE CUSTOMER, NOT STATEMENTS

TSRs need to do many things when they are selling a product over the telephone. Two of those things are first, to maintain the customer's interest in the product and then second, to keep the conversation moving. I believe that the best way to accomplish both of these goals is to have the customer ask questions of the TSR. I touched upon this earlier by saying that if the customer is asking questions, then the customer is demonstrating that he is very interested in what he has been hearing and that he wants the TSR to inform him with regard to some new items, as well. It also means, more to the point, that the TSR has established credibility with the customer. I train TSRs to make a slash mark on a piece of scratch paper each time the customer asks them a question in the conversation. There is no set number of questions that usually lead to completed sales, but hearing questions being asked always sets off a bell in my mind. There is nothing more flattering to a TSR, and more worthwhile, than to hear a customer say "I want to be informed, and I want you to be the informer."

**TELE-TIP**

When customers start saying things such as "I got that part" or "You mentioned that already" or "I understand, I understand", the TSR should realize the sale is drifting away.

How can TSRs encourage their customers to ask questions? When selling over the telephone, I have found two distinct styles to be the best ways to encourage and motivate customers to ask questions over the telephone.

## 1. Ask Customers One Dynamic Question

"Mr. Customer, what questions do you have for me?"

Simple and effective, this is a telling question to ask over the telephone. If the customer has no questions to ask, then the TSR is either ready to close and complete the sale, or the TSR will probably lose the sale because the customer is not interested.

Other variations of this question that can be asked over the telephone include:

"Ms. Customer, do you have any questions for me?"

"Ms. Customer, I've asked many questions. What questions do you have for me?"

"Now it is your turn Mr. Customer. What three questions can I answer for you?"

"Are there three things I haven't touched upon that you would like to know?"

"Boy, it seems like we have covered everything. What did I miss?"

"Before we continue, are there any other questions I can answer?"

## 2. Provide Thought-Provoking Conversation

We have all participated in two types of conversations. One type sparks the imagination and interest of all parties so that they want to hear and participate more. The second type of conversation is unimaginative, without thought, not constructive, and discourages all parties from listening. There is no question that by sparking the imagination and interest of the customer, the TSR has a far greater opportunity to draw questions from the customer. In addition, TSRs have the ability to draw questions from customers when they begin to manipulate their dialogue and open up their dialogue to encourage questions. A TSR can do this by not finishing his sentences completely, or by exploring a topic and then changing direction suddenly, leaving the customer <u>wanting to know</u>. When the TSR does these things, the customer immediately becomes interested in what *was* being communicated. The Los Angeles Times had a fascinating advertising campaign going on in 1995, 1996, and 1997, utilizing just this technique. On radio and television, in print and on billboards, the Los Angeles Times displayed about four sentences of a story with the ending cut off. Clearly, the missing points were the most interesting and telling points of the story. In telephone sales, inquisitive customers who find themselves faced with missing endings ask the TSR questions to find out the ends of sentences. Hence, stopping sentences when they are getting interesting or leaving subjects incomplete when selling over the telephone may work well if this technique manipulates the customer into asking questions so he can learn more. When designing their advertising, the intent of the Los Angeles Times was not to focus on one particular story. In fact, most of the four sentences came from general stories completely outdated. The intent was to spark one question from their customer base: "I wonder what I am missing when I am not reading the Los Angeles Times. I'd better purchase a newspaper." In the same manner, the intent of the telephone sales representative is to motivate the customer to say "I wonder what I am missing. I'd better ask a question."

## TONE, PACE, INFLECTION, MELODY

We have all been in the same situation at one time or another. A classroom. A large class. A dull professor. The question to ask is "What makes the professor dull?" The same things that make a professor dull oftentimes make a TSR dull. The most common reason professors are dull is because the subject matter is boring. Perhaps the students have little or no interest in the subject matter, and they project their lack of interest to the professor. (This also explains why some students think a professor is better than others think he is.) Another reason professors are dull is because they, as repeaters of the same subject class after class, week after week, month after month, and year after year, have lost the pizzazz to deliver successful lectures. Although the students are hearing a particular lecture for the first time, professors transfer their boredom to the students in quite the same way the students project their boredom onto their professors.

**TELE-TIP**

There is no set number of questions that usually lead to completed sales, but hearing questions being asked always sets off a bell in my mind.

Clearly, the jobs of TSRs and professors, in these instances, are analogous. TSRs can fall upon the trap of complacency and forget that each customer is hearing the presentation for the very first time. TSRs oftentimes can't comprehend why a customer doesn't understand a point, only to realize that the customer hasn't heard this point as strongly and persuasively as the last customer heard it. Conversely, customers can become quickly indifferent to the subject matter the TSR is delivering, and may project this indifference upon the TSR, although the TSR has had little or no opportunity to rescue the presentation.

In order to keep the above situations from occurring and to increase the odds of successful telephone sales presentations, I want to spend some time explaining the use of tone, pace, inflection and melody as they relate to the telephone sales call. By successfully portraying wonderful tone, pace, inflection and melody at the right moments and in the correct ways, the TSR will have the ability to more easily utilize all the concepts presented in this book. Presentations that might not be moving in the desired direction often turn around completely with proper use of tone, pace, inflection and melody. Finally, sentences will become more defined, clearer, and make more of an impact on the customer. These four elements of a telephone call are critical steps to becoming a top TSR.

It is important to remember that tone, pace, inflection and melody work as well with one another as without, depending on situational use. Although these four elements are commonly tossed together as if they were one complete package, it is mandatory that TSRs use each element to its maximum potential. I, for example, am awful when it comes to portraying wonderful melody over the telephone, but I am outstanding at presenting tone and inflection. So, while I attempt to sell the complete package, I always concentrate on how my tone and inflection sound when I sell over the telephone. To help the TSR better understand exactly what tone, pace, inflection and melody are and how they work when communicating over the telephone, I have listed below some of the things and people we associate with tone, pace, inflection and melody:

Musicians

Music

Actors

Singers

Dogs

Piano

Ear Piercing Noise

Speed

High and Low Notes

Expression of Meaning

I provide the above examples to illustrate a special point. Becoming a successful telephone sales representative can be accomplished when the TSR utilizes much of the same areas that make *sounds* such an important part of our everyday lives. Computer generated sounds, musical sounds, sounds from a friend or relative, etc. A part of human nature nobody can dispute is that the sounds that make all of us happy are sounds we enjoy, and the sounds that make all of us sad are sounds we dislike. <u>Selling over the phone very much involves creating sounds that make all of us happy</u>. Even if TSRs communicate *words* that should make customers happy, the customers won't respond to those words unless they are presented with analogous sounds to establish their credibility. This harks back to a previous chapter (<u>Understanding Telephone Selling</u>) when I talked about *how* and it's importance to *what*. The *how* that the TSR must sell is equivalent to the sounds he must communicate, whereas the *what* that the TSR must sell (far less important) are the words the TSR communicates. For example, suppose the owner of a dog sits down next to the dog and says in his most trusting and friendly and loving tone "You are the ugliest and most stupid dog, and I hate you very much." The words spoken are horrible, they are the "What" of the presentation. If the dog were to respond to the words alone, the dog would be put in a sad and disapproving state. The dog would be unhappy with its owner. However, the tone in which the words are presented is, as I mentioned, a trusting and friendly and loving tone. These words are the "How" of the presentation.

What will the dog's reaction be?

The dog will love the owner's sentence. The dog will respond positively to the sentence. The dog will probably jump up and down, lick the owner's face, and ask for more.

This example illustrates the importance of tone in a telephone sales call. *"How"* a sentence is delivered makes all of the difference in the way that sentence is received. Bosses who have successfully terminated relationships with employees base much of their successful handling of such events on "how" they deliver the poor news. TSRs have a golden opportunity to complete many more telephone sales calls by dynamically mastering the tone in which they present their product. Two sentences, delivered verbatim word-by-word, but presented in different tones, will generally receive different responses from the customer.

## WHICH TONE SELLS?

There are only two types of tones that make a difference when communicating and selling over the telephone. One type sells effectively over the telephone, the other one does not. Before we explore these two tones, one meaningful note. It is important for the telephone sales representative to recognize that a slippage and transfer from one tone to another will always jeopardize the possibilities of success, because the customer can assume three things from a slippage or change in tone:

The TSR is changing his sales presentation for an unknown reason

The TSR is losing confidence in his own presentation

The TSR is not a person the customer can feel comfortable with

In other words, consistency is paramount for the TSR when he applies his tone to the conversation. Once that tone is established, it is nearly impossible for the TSR to eliminate the established tone and substitute a new one because a multitude of other aspects have become established as well. All of these aspects impact the TSR's credibility. Remain consistent!

The first type of tone, and the one the TSR should always stay away from, is a high tone, or high pitch. I call this the Patrick Buchanan / School Principal tone, because it is the one tone that turns people off. <u>From a customer's perspective, the customer needs to feel secure in the TSR's credibility, and a high tone takes any security away</u>. Customers associate a high tone over the phone with slippery sales makers. When customers hear a TSR with a high tone selling a product over the telephone, they visualize sweaty brows and beady eyes. As I mentioned in an earlier chapter, telephone selling is a verbal medium where the TSR visually demonstrates his presentation in order to complete the sale. It is unfortunate but true that customers do not receive a great visual demonstration from a high pitched TSR.

The second element of tone, and the one the TSR should attempt to present to the customer, is a low tone, or low pitch. I call this the Radio Newscaster / Public Address Announcer tone, because this tone attracts customers with its sincerity and comfort. <u>Customers trust telephone sales representatives who project a low tone</u>. Throughout the history of radio, many of the truly successful newscasters who delivered life breaking news had low, comfortable and steady voices that encouraged listeners to turn up their radios and trust that what they were hearing was true. The voice that sells a low tone is the one that soothes the customer. The visual demonstration is positive.

## PACE

I was once asked how many times I heard a telephone sales conversation sound like a race between two competing factions. My response was that I hear this all of the time, and it drives me mad. For example, instead of communicating *together*, the TSR and customer tend to get into the throes of communicating their points and ideas *on top of* one another, causing stilted conversation and a lack of coherency. This lack of pace will sink a telephone sales call all of the time, and it is the job of a very good TSR to realize how important pace is when it comes to establishing credibility in a phone call.

It is critical for TSRs to learn and understand how each telephone call has a certain pace to it. For example, perhaps the customer is in a hurry and wants to speed everything up. In that case, the TSR should use a quick pace as well as a fast rhythm. On the flip side, perhaps the TSR can establish a pace with the customer (which the customer accepts) that moves the conversation in a plodding, almost analytical style of listening, talking, theorizing, and contemplating. In that case, the pace of the call has been designed to promote a very methodical style of selling, and the TSR should beware of any fluctuation.

When TSRs try to apply pace to the business of selling, they can see some ready analogies. Before the Indy 500, there is a pace car that all the other cars follow. This pace car keeps the flow and rhythm of the race on the correct course. In a horse race, the excitement of watching the horses run down the stretch is assisted by the PA announcer, who provides the statuses of where the horses are in relation to the race. Certainly, horse racing is exciting without the PA announcer, but the announcer is a critical link in establishing the pace of each race. "DOWN THE STRETCH THEY COME!!!"

I believe establishing pace is important for two main reasons: so the customer feels he is more a part of the presentation, and so the presentation comes off in a smooth and compelling way, enabling the TSR to more easily complete the sale.

In this light, TSRs must take the following five steps to successfully establish and utilize pace to their advantage throughout a telephone sales call:

**TELE-TIP**

TSRs can fall upon the trap of complacency and forget that each customer is hearing the presentation for the very first time. TSRs oftentimes can't comprehend why a customer doesn't understand a point, only to realize that the customer hasn't heard this point as strongly and persuasively as the last customer heard it.

1. **TSRs Must Set the Pace to Their Levels**

   If the TSR can set the pace of the telephone call, then the TSR has made a successful stab at controlling the direction of the call. The TSR has said "Here is the pace in which I will deliver this presentation to you." The customer has agreed to relinquish control.

2. **TSRs Must Set A Comfortable Pace for the Customer**

   If the TSR is unable to set the pace to his level, then it is mandatory that he set the pace to his customer's level. Comfortable pace, no matter who controls it, is critical. Fighting for control of the pace when the TSR can't win is a losing proposition. Like any good battle tactician, if the TSR is unable to win pace, then he must settle for establishing any pace he can.

3. **TSRs Must Sustain Consistency**

   TSRs have the tendency to lose sales because they get over-eager to close sales when customers aren't quite ready. On the other hand, when a customer speeds up the pace, it becomes foolish for the TSR to try to maintain a past consistency. Instead, the TSR needs to find the new pace of the call and establish that consistency.

4. **TSRs Must Perform**

   In a sense, customers say "yes" to a sales offer when they have been entertained and when they enjoy what they have heard. A stand-up comedian on stage gets his audience to say "yes" to a dynamite performance when the comedian is able to coordinate the pace of his presentation to his audience. Listen to successful comedians talk about the results of their shows. If they were able to get a good pace developed with the audience, the show was usually a success. TSRs must concentrate on getting customers involved with the presentation. If they can't do that, then the presentation is "off-pace" and is not appealing to the customer.

5. **TSRs Must Learn The Elements Of Pace**

   Speaking quickly versus speaking slowly.

   Emphasizing main points decisively versus emphasizing main points methodically.

   Using humor versus not using humor.

   Asking simple questions versus asking detailed questions.

   Presenting a litany of benefits versus introducing one benefit at a time.

   In the last forty years, I have found no person who epitomizes the importance of pace better than Los Angeles Dodgers' sports broadcaster Vin Scully. Those who have heard Scully recognize his play-by-play delivery to be the best in the business. Why? Because every game is broadcast consistently. Each inning, even each sentence, is comfortable to listen to and easy to understand.

Also, Scully has the best knack for *establishing* pace of any sports broadcaster I have ever heard. It is Scully's unparalleled ability to master pace throughout a sports broadcast that separates him from most every other sports broadcaster in the business. In contrast to Scully, many other sports broadcasters have severe difficulty maintaining a quality pace in a baseball game. And this difficulty severs any chance of a good, solid, comfortable relationship between sports broadcaster and fan. Why do sports broadcasters have such a difficult time with pace? Primarily, the action of the game throws them for a loop. (This same dilemma challenges TSRs, who often become thrown for a loop during the action of a telephone sales call.) One inning, an announcer may be speaking with perfect pace, perfect enough that the lis-

**TELE-TIP**

Even if TSRs communicate words that should make customers happy, the customers won't respond to those words unless they are presented with analogous sounds to establish their credibility.

tener over the radio gets into a rhythm, and a beat, with the broadcaster. They are tuned into one another, and that fine-tuning enhances the fan's listening enjoyment. This is what every sports broadcaster, and every TSR, hopes to accomplish. Seconds later, however, the sports broadcaster loses his pace. Perhaps he takes extra long pauses between pitches. Perhaps the sports broadcaster starts and stops a story with such inconsistency that one feels

like he is listening to a driver trying to orchestrate a clutch on a 1968 Rambler American for the first time. Perhaps the score is read consistently for a while, then not updated for minutes at a time. Perhaps the balls and strikes, once called evenly, become stilted barbs as the sports broadcaster falls behind. Whatever the challenge, 90% of all the sports broadcasters who deliver baseball games today can't sustain a consistent pace, and that makes listening to their broadcasts a very rocky process.

Problems with pace, like those mentioned above, don't happen very often, if at all, to Vin Scully. Each pitch is called by Scully with a crispness of pace over the course of all nine innings. Telling stories is Scully's forte, and each story is relayed entertainingly and sharply to the fan, with little or no action missed. Scully's fine-tuning and steady pace keeps the fan involved. Clearly, I would be expecting too much if I demanded that every TSR have the same skill level when delivering pace as Vin Scully. On the other hand, the principles of pace that make Scully a true Hall-Of-Fame sports broadcaster can be applied to TSRs who want to be the best in their business.

In both instances (sports announcing and telephone selling) the communicator is dealing with an audience. That audience is always different in nature, but all audiences, even different in nature, demand the same things from their communicator. They demand consistency in the presentation, and a presentation that they can latch onto, expecting constant pace from start to finish.

## INFLECTION

I once had a girlfriend I was crazy about, but the detriment to our relationship was that we couldn't communicate with one another. Boy, was that frustrating! Every time she communicated with me she utilized a different tone, and I never could completely figure out how she really felt about me. It was frustrating. Every time we had long conversations, our pace would be off from one another. I would speak quickly, she would speak slowly, and nothing would get accomplished. Most distressing, however, was the fact that when she spoke, she utilized *inflection* absolutely terribly. I was utterly confused as to what she needed and what she wanted, because when she spoke, she inflected her words incorrectly. It was this terrible use of inflection that added to the confusion of our relationship and finally caused us to split up.

I deliver this depressing bit of personal history to illustrate how necessary the use of good inflection can be to a telephone sales presentation. Since customers can't see the TSR, they must rely completely on their senses (primarily the sense of hearing). So, if the TSR chooses to present a humorous anecdote to the customer without first making it clear through inflection that the anecdote is humorous, this can backfire on the TSR and jeopardize the sale. In outside sales the attempt might work because the customer would see facial expressions, hand movements and incidentals that would demonstrate the humor involved in the anecdote. Over the phone, however, the TSR's ability to tell a good joke is at the mercy of his ability to inflect the joke successfully to the customer.

We spoke about comedians before. Much of their presentation centers around the wonderful use of tone, pace, inflection and melody. Comedians will probably say, however, that the proper use of inflection in a presentation is the key ingredient of a successful comedy presentation. On television, we can see how important inflection is to a presentation. After Jay Leno or David Letterman or Conan O' Brien delivers a punch line, his proper

**TELE-TIP**

Consistency is paramount for the TSR when he applies his tone to the conversation. Once that tone is established, it is nearly impossible for the TSR to eliminate the established tone and substitute a new one because a multitude of other aspects have become established as well.

**TELE-TIP**

Listen to successful comedians talk about the results of their shows. If they were able to get a good pace developed with the audience, the show was usually a success.

use of inflection either makes or breaks the joke. If it is good, the band will accompany the joke with some sort of musical piece, which almost always adds to the joke. If it is good, the audience will pick up exactly what the comedian is trying to express, and find the punch line to be humorous. If it's bad, however…

This is why TSRs are under extreme pressure to master inflection. TSRs are at the mercy of their customers' perceptions. If a customer perceives that a sentence is funny, he will laugh, even if the TSR makes a mistake with his inflection and doesn't expect the customer to laugh. Humor is very good in a presentation, and a customer's laughter is nearly always positive. On the other hand, if customers don't find a sentence humorous or if customers don't laugh when they should because of the improper use of inflection by the TSR, then the TSR finds himself in a hole. Customers' perceptions are such tricky things to manage that the only way to even *attempt* to manage them is to communicate each sentence exactly the way the TSR wants that sentence to be communicated. How to deliver inflection on words is a fundamental decision for the TSR, on every call. One sentence can be construed by the customer to mean a hundred different things depending on how the TSR inflects his words.

"I DID NOT SAY HE ATE THE FOOD"

"**I** did not say he ate the food!"

"I **did** not say he ate the food!"

"I did **not** say he ate the food!"

"I did not **say** he ate the food!"

"I did not say **he** ate the food!"

"I did not say he **ate** the food?????"

"I did not say he ate **the** food!"

"I did not say he ate the **food**?????"

"**I did not say he ate the food?**"

"**I did not say he ate the food!**"

"I did not say he ate the food."

"I DID NOT SAY HE ATE THE FOOD!"

The above example illustrates all of the possible ways in which one sentence may be delivered. Clearly, each sentence may be construed to mean something different from all the rest. Hence, "How" the TSR inflects his words will explain to the customer exactly "What" messages the TSR is attempting to communicate.

When communicating over the telephone, there are a few words in the English language that the TSR can always rely on to make his point.

---

### THE CHILDREN'S BOOKS SELLING EXAMPLE

*If the TSR wants to emphasize the involvement of a particular person, the TSR should generate inflection on his pronouns in order to make the sentence more pronounced:*

"**I** think you should buy these children's books!"

"**We** are in agreement your kids will enjoy the books, right?"

"**You** have told me you spend lots of money on books, correct?"

"**He** had mentioned that you are the decision maker."

"**They** always find that the books have wonderful pictures."

"**She** said she wasn't interested, didn't she?"

*If the TSR wants to emphasize the involvement of a particular person, place or thing, the TSR should generate inflection on his nouns in order to make the sentence more pronounced:*

"**Larry** didn't want to order the six book set."

"The best way to make the purchase is **by phone**, don't you agree?"

"I believe the best thing about **books** is that they are long lasting and durable."

"She wasn't going to look at the books until **George** told her to do so."

"**Western Alabama** is the region of the country with the highest number of orders. Did you know?"

*If the TSR wants to emphasize a wonderful aspect of the program, the TSR should generate inflection on his adjectives in order to make the sentence more pronounced:*

"Mr. Smith, do very **beautiful** children's books appeal to your girls?"

---

### MELODY

We have explored three of the four ways to communicate the actual words and sentences and ideas of a presentation to the customer (tone, pace and inflection). The fourth way of communicating actual words, sentences and ideas is through the utilization of melody. For me, this aspect is the most fun, and therefore I find it the easiest to teach.

**TELE-TIP**

Over the phone however, the TSR's ability to tell a good joke is at the mercy of his ability to inflect the joke successfully to the customer.

Communicating melody over the telephone can very much be accomplished by communicating the presentation to the customer in a style that represents music. Melody is the "bounce" in a telephone sales presentation that makes the presentation worth listening to. In essence, the melody of a presentation is the combination of tone, pace and inflection, all rolled into a lively and pleasurable environment.

I am a firm believer in music as it relates to motivating people to act and do things. (How many times have we heard a song on the radio that so captured our emotions that it gave us the incentive to do something?) Perhaps the phrase "Melody is the music that soothes the savage beast" sounds familiar. Since telephone selling is about motivating the customer to act and to do something, the TSR must be responsible for creating a melody in his presentation that gives the customer an incentive to act. For example, some product presentations, and TSRs, work best when the melody of the presentation duplicates a rock n' roll environment- quick, crazy, fast paced. The TSR may take on the voice of a 60's disc jockey, as he sings his presentation to the customer in that way to which they *both* relate.

Try imagining listening to a favorite song without the melody. It would sound pretty miserable. True, the words would be the same words that helped make that song a favorite song. But, without proper melody from the singer, the song loses its appeal. Words by themselves can't do the trick. Now, try listening to a remake of a favorite song. So often the remake is even <u>better</u> than the original. This is because, even though the words stay the same, the melody has been changed, upgraded by the musicians and singers to make more of an impact with the audience.

It is imperative to generate a strong melody over the telephone, in order to capture the customer. Some TSRs have that intangible way of singing their words to the customer in a way that captivates the customer; other telephone sales reps couldn't manipulate a melody in a million years, and they struggle to convey even simple messages.

One musical celebrity who communicates melody to her audience particularly well is Alanyss Morrisett. Morrisett had a plethora of top singles in

1995 and 1996, and her songs carry a melody that truly separates her music from the works of others. Not only do her words convey a message to her audience, but the melody she presents does more to explain what her songs mean than anything else. In addition, most fans consider her melodies to be all over the place. No musician in modern music can carry tone, pace and inflection like she can, and this is what very much has added to her success.

## CUSTOMERS' VIEWS OF TSR CREDIBILITY

As we discussed in the beginning of this chapter, TSRs often make the fatal mistake of thinking they have established credibility with their customers when they haven't. The important thing to remember is that only one person, the customer, determines TSR credibility. The customer is judge and jury wrapped into one. Only the thought processes of the customer count.

Below are the six areas where customers judge a TSR's credibility:

1. **Customers Perceive *Who* the TSR Is**

   Is the TSR looking out for the best interest of himself, his customer, his company, or all three?

2. **Customers Perceive *What* the TSR Is**

   Is the TSR spending his days sitting by himself in a garage, pulling a scam, or does the TSR represent himself appropriately? Is the TSR what he says he is?

3. **Customers Perceive *The Purpose* Of The TSR's Telephone Call**

   Is the TSR out to sell a product, gather information for a database, pre-screen customers for another TSR, etc?

4. **Customers Perceive What TSRs *Need* From The Telephone Call**

   Customers perceive whether the TSRs need decisions right off the bat, money, or future agreements to hear more about the offer later.

5. **Customers Perceive What The TSR's *Product* Encompasses**

   Is the product worth the customers' time?

6. **Customers Perceive *What* the TSR'S Product Offers *Them***

   Will the product benefit the customer?

## SKILLS NEEDED TO ENHANCE CREDIBILITY

● **Accumulate Product Knowledge**

   The TSR must take time away from the office to study the product he is going to sell. He must make notes that he can bring back to the office and utilize while he is on the telephone. The TSR must take the time to think about what makes his particular program tick, and how he can present the strengths of his program credibly.

> *Take a notebook and jot down every single piece of information about the product. Separate the notebook by subject matter. The TSR should keep the notebook by his desk for simple reference. Never throw away the notebook. Never discard the notebook. The accessibility of the notebook is what separates telephone sales reps from outside sales reps.*

To further examine this situation, imagine for a moment that the TSR has been asked to teach a class, yet never gave any thought at all to the subject matter. The TSR wouldn't appear to be very credible to the class. Now imagine that the TSR went to a class as a guest lecture speaker but had no information on the subject he had come to talk about. In both cases the TSR is the expert, and it is the TSR who caused his own predicament. In the former, he chose to teach a class. In the latter, he chose to be a guest speaker. But in each situation he was unprepared. The telephone sales representative had no credibility because he had undertaken little preparation with regard to the details of his product. I have seen a lack of credibility affect TSRs millions of times every day. The image of telephone sales has taken dramatic beatings in the media and throughout society due to the few people in this industry who do not do their jobs correctly. They have now placed the burden on the TSR to present his product as credibly as possible in order to alleviate customer concerns.

## ● Understand TSR Weaknesses

It should never be a problem for a TSR to admit to the customer his weaknesses or his product's weaknesses, as long as these are presented in the appropriate context.   For example, one weakness may be that the TSR is brand new at the job. The TSR can let the customer know this! Perhaps his product is a discounted magazine, but the magazine does not have any scientific articles in it. When the customer asks if there are scientific articles in the magazine, the TSR should not be shy in letting him know that it does not have those articles. However, the TSR should be efficient in explaining why. Most often, telephone sales reps see weaknesses as their downfall, as if once the customer discovers one weakness the sale will be over. The TSR can humanize himself and his product and gain credibility with the customer by admitting his weaknesses succinctly, turning them into positives, and demonstrating why they do not affect the offer.

## ● Ask the Right Questions

In the following pages we will go into more detail regarding asking questions of the customer. Needless to say, most telephone sales reps do not ask enough questions of their customers to uncover their needs, and they end up presenting a product or an aspect of a product that does not have any benefit to the customer. This causes a loss of credibility points. Telephone sales reps must ask questions of their customers so certain things will be accomplished. *First*, questions get the customer involved in the call. If the telephone sales rep presents a question, the customer is obliged to answer it, and that might open up a conversation and cause camaraderie to develop between the two parties. *Second*, questions help the telephone sales rep ascertain needs. Telephone sales reps never come off as if they are credible when they attempt to sell something the customer has no need for. By asking questions, the telephone sales rep can discover what the customer needs. *Third*, questions help the TSR to express legitimacy to the customer. The customer will get a sense of what the program is about if the TSR asks him questions that get him to talk to the TSR about a particular subject. If the TSR is selling insurance and asks four questions about insurance, the customer will feel comfortable because he will know exactly where the TSR is coming from.

# TELE-TIP

Since telephone selling is about motivating the customer to act and to do something, the TSR must be responsible for creating a melody in his presentation that gives the customer an incentive to act.

## ● Have the Answers Fast

Having answers fast demonstrates to the customer that the TSR is both a professional telephone sales representative as well as a dedicated person trying his best to sell the program. I have actually monitored calls where the customer would have said "yes" to an offer and bought the product if only the telephone sales rep had sounded half-way knowledgeable and interested in supplying quality answers to the customer's questions. If a customer asks a question, he is ready to buy, or at least is demonstrating interest in a possible buy. It is the telephone sales rep's job to take that question and give the customer a credible and strong response. Anything less will tell the customer that the TSR doesn't want the sale badly enough to persuade him to say "yes".

As in other areas of telephone sales, the TSR needs to use his creativity to develop a rock solid rapport with the customer. The way to do this is to remain himself, which means he should always portray himself over the phone as if he were talking to a friend in a nice and casual conversation. We trust our friends, and we trust people who are open and honest about themselves. When the TSR uses the right words and expresses the benefits of his product in a positive manner, the customer gets a warm and positive feeling about the program.

## ● Utilize Verbals and Sounds in an Appropriate Manner

We already learned all about tone, pace, inflection and melody. By remaining cognizant of the fact that telephone selling is a verbal medium that involves hitting the correct tone, pace, inflection and melody at the appropriate times, the TSR will make huge strides in his ability to communicate credibly to his customer.

## ● Mimic The Customer

I stress throughout this book that the TSR should be creative and unique on the telephone. One way to go about this is to sound just like the person you are talking with, which- on the face of it- may sound very non-creative and non-unique. Sound just like him? How will I be able to gain his attention and capture his imagination and involve him if I don't put on a show? Mimicking the customer is sometimes the best way to accomplish all of the above, because it makes the customer as comfortable as possible with the TSR. When I talk about mimicking, I certainly don't mean that the TSR should repeat verbatim what the customer says, or make the customer feel self-conscious or conspicuous about his comments. Mimicking the customer centers primarily around the tone, pace, inflection and melody that the customer uses when communicating with the TSR. If the customer is a fast talker, it is best for the TSR to talk fast, so the customer is listening and hearing the TSR at his most comfortable level. Accordingly, if the customer speaks in a monotone and provides no inflection in his questions and statements, the TSR should do the same. Communicating inflection to a customer who doesn't use it can quickly intimidate the customer and place him on the defensive. Customers, as human beings, are most comfortable with people like themselves, and they tend to be responsive to the TSR when they feel that they are communicating with a similar personality.

The TSR can humanize himself and his product and gain credibility with the customer by admitting his weaknesses succinctly, turning them into positives, and demonstrating why they do not affect the offer.

# CHAPTER

# PRESENTATION LEVELS

As we have undoubtedly discovered, in the course of a telephone sales presentation there are many roads for the TSR and the customer to embark upon. These roads are very similar to the roads which each of us take each day in the performance of our daily activities. From the moment a person awakes in the morning until that person lays down to sleep at night, the whole day is full of roads that incorporate twists, turns, obstacles and barriers. Encounters that start at one level eventually conclude at another, but the path we take on a daily basis is never consistent or even as we envisioned it would be. The course of a telephone sales presentation mimics the above in every way. From the moment a TSR dials the telephone, through the instant of communication and until the telephone call is terminated, every step of the way is charted through multiple roads, full of twists, turns, obstacles and barriers. I call these roads *telephone presentation levels*, because each step in a telephone sales presentation moves that call forward and backward through multiple presentation levels. Presentation levels form the path that a TSR takes to complete his sale.

An outstanding telephone sales presentation is very much similar to a great race through a maze. If the TSR is good at his job he will be able to figure out what he wants to accomplish and where he needs to go, both prior to the beginning of the telephone presentation and then through its inception and on to its conclusion. In effect, I analogize a TSR making a presentation to the example of a mouse avoiding land traps as the mouse maneuvers his way around a house. The mouse is the TSR while the house is a telephone sales presentation. Things look promising if the mouse has the ability and knows what he is doing. However, it's quite a long way from one end of the house to the other and, unfortunately for both the mouse and the TSR, getting caught is never a good thing.

As we have explored in other chapters, the key to a completed telephone sales presentation is the mixture of the bits and pieces that combine to form a dynamite presentation. The presentation is the backbone of the call, because what the TSR communicates in the presentation will always, under every circumstance, make or break each call. But telephone presentations are not a constant and they are not simple. A presentation over the telephone can begin in one location and zip through as many as thirty or forty different ports before the call is finally concluded. These ports are the presentation levels of a telephone sales call. At each step of the way, the presentation level needs to be mastered by the TSR to the best of his ability before he can approach the next level, conquer it, and then move on. Every time the telephone presentation moves from one subject to the next, one presentation level has ended, and another presentation level has begun.

From the moment a TSR dials the telephone, through the instant of communication and until the telephone call is terminated, every step of the way is charted through multiple roads, full of twists, turns, obstacles and barriers. I call these roads telephone presentation levels.

Because every presentation to a customer will consist of countless numbers of presentation levels, the mathematical chance of achieving success and making sales improves greatly the more times the TSR utilizes his presentation levels and presents the program to the customer. The correct notion that pursuing sales over and over and over again in order to complete sales is a constant of selling which never fluctuates. Perseverance is the only way TSRs become successful. Moving the presentation through the many presentation levels of a call is the way to make money.

Let's look at an analogy. When one decides it is time to go on a diet to lose weight, he understands that the only way to truly achieve success is to pursue various stages of the diet. Similarly, when one decides to close a sale over the telephone, he understands that the only way to truly achieve success is to pursue various stages of his presentation levels. For a dieter, losing the first five pounds may come very easily because he needs to remain on the diet for only a short period of time to accomplish that goal. But reaching the paramount goal of losing thirty pounds can become tremendously difficult for a dieter, for no other reason except that the deeper one goes into pursuing a diet, the more variables accumulate to make remaining on the diet extremely difficult. In that same way, telephone sales representatives should understand that getting a quick sale happens usually through luck and doesn't happen very often. The way to complete many sales is to move more deeply into conversation with the customers. A dieter understands <u>reflectively</u> that he will lose weight if he stays on course and goes through the different levels of the diet. But the dieter also acts <u>reactively</u> to the fact that it is much simpler and easier and more enjoyable in any short term of five seconds or five minutes to just eat and break the diet and start over the next time. In like manner, TSRs understand <u>reflectively</u> that they should pursue each call until they run out of presentation levels to do so. Unfortunately, during the <u>reaction</u> of a telephone presentation, TSRs tend to end the call early in the hope of moving on to another call and finding better luck. In essence, dieting and telephone sales are both nothing more than the act of pursuing when it is easier not to, the challenge of staying with a disciplined objective when it is easier to lose focus, and the handling of impromptu intangibles while fighting from one level to the next.

Below are tips to successfully utilize presentation levels:

● **Presentation Levels In A Telephone Call Are Infinite**

Each call has its own number of presentation levels. Some telephone calls that last ten minutes or so may span twenty or thirty presentation levels, while other calls may encounter only five or six.

● **Perseverance of Presentation Levels Completes Sales**

The TSR must never give up on a telephone sales call. Because 80% of all sales are completed by only 20% of all sales reps, those 20% have demonstrated that consistent pursuing pays dividends.

● **Presentation Levels Give the TSR A Distinct Advantage**

The more times a TSR can move the presentation past its various levels, the better chance the TSR has of completing the sale. If the customer moves through the different levels with the TSR, the customer is demonstrating interest, and every presentation level where the TSR can cultivate that interest is a bonus.

● **Understanding Presentation Levels Will Give Direction to the Telephone Call**

Each presentation level is a different road. During a telephone call, the TSR can map out the roads he has already traveled and the roads he needs to travel in order to control the direction of the telephone sales call and eventually close the sale.

## SCRIPTING DIFFERENT LEVELS IN A TELEPHONE SALES PRESENTATION

A few areas must be defined clearly to understand presentation levels. As we noted, the number of presentation levels in an *actual* sales presentation can be infinite. For example, each level can involve asking and receiving an answer to a question, or continuous closing and negotiating on a certain topic. In this respect, a presentation can go on for hours and involve a thousand separate levels, or it can last five minutes and involve the traditional seven scripted levels we will learn about below. Because each presentation takes on a world of its own, it is literally impossible to set forth guidelines of what should or should not be a valid presentation. <u>Also, although there can be a variety of levels in a telephone presentation, all TSRs must recognize that there are only seven overriding presentation levels which should be scripted during a telephone sales presentation.</u> Seven! Hence, when either designing telephone sales scripts, teaching scripting, or formulating a telephone sales game plan, I let TSRs know clearly that all telephone sales scripts can easily be predicated upon seven levels. Can scripting a telephone presentation be more complicated than seven levels? Absolutely, but more complicated doesn't mean better. (I commonly see consultants provide twenty- level scripts that fail miserably!) When I draft scripts for telephone sales projects, I maintain for my client the seven- level format. I do this for three reasons. *First,* because good TSRs normally develop combinations of the company's script and their own script anyhow, and use the official script as a mere guide to better selling. *Second,* because great telephone sales scripts should be flexible for the TSR, and anything that encompasses more than seven levels begins to bog the TSR down during the presentation.. *Third,* because seven presentation levels in a script work, providing the TSR with all the ammunition he needs to close sales and increase his production! The signifi-

**TELE-TIP**

The correct notion that pursuing sales over and over and over again in order to complete sales is a constant of selling which never fluctuates. Perseverance is the only way TSRs become successful.

cant aspect of presentation levels is that there is a difference between what happens in the presentation and the process of scripting a presentation. What happens in a presentation borders on controlled chaos, where only the adaptable TSR will survive. Scripting a presentation relies upon developing a solid framework to guide the TSR and customer while providing a basic structure for the TSR to follow as he enters the presentation level maze.

Below is a rundown of the seven levels of a scripted presentation with directions on what each of the levels tries to accomplish.

1.  **Introduction**

    INTRODUCE the TSR and his product to the customer

    INVOLVE the customer in the conversation

    PERSUADE the customer to have confidence in the presentation

    MOTIVATE the customer to want to listen to the presentation

2. **Qualification**

   ENSURE the customer is eligible for the program

   LISTEN to the customer to identify want he wants / needs

   GAUGE which benefits and features work best with each customer

3. **Probes**

   ASK questions to find out what the customer needs / wants

   INTERPRET which aspects of the program will best sell the program

   IDENTIFY answers and use those answers to formulate sales assisting questions

4. **Benefits and Features**

   EXPLAIN product benefits so the customer understands the program

   INFLUENCE the customer

   DEFINE how the customer could benefit in the future from the program

   SUPPORT benefits with constructive features that illustrate the product's strength

5. **Trial Closing**

   PERSUADE the customer to say yes

   CONDITION the customer to recognize the benefits of the program

   CLASSIFY aspects of the telephone presentation which work from those that don't

6. **Handling Objections**

   AGREE that what the customer is saying is true

   SQUELCH the customer's fears with a persuasive answer

   STIMULATE the customer to understand why your rebuttal may be accurate

   ASK questions of the customer to find information and increase rapport

   EMPLOY outstanding hearing skills to discern answers and generate a response

7. **Closing**

   DECIDE when to close or when to trial close again

   FINISH the presentation

   ENCOURAGE agreement on the direction and results of the presentation

## INTRODUCTION AND QUALIFICATION

It is pretty much agreed upon by industry experts that the introduction of a telephone sales presentation and the qualification of a customer are two important elements to the presentation. Certainly, every element is important, but introduction and qualification are especially important for two reasons. *First,* because the introduction and the qualification are the first two aspects of a presentation which the customer hears. *Second,* because in almost all instances it is at the introduction and qualification that the entire stage is set for the way in which the rest of the telephone call is going to proceed.

## INTRODUCTION

The introduction of the TSR's presentation is the first segment of communication that the customer hears. When two different parties meet one another for the first time, there is always an element of friction that develops. To ensure the telephone presentation is successful, this friction must become positive. To do this successfully, the TSR must establish in his telephone introduction seven objectives and utilize these seven objectives completely.

### 1. The Introduction Should Have Direction

An introduction is successful when the TSR knows where he wants to go with the introduction and what is required to get there. If the TSR appears indecisive or confused in the introduction, the customer will feel the same way, and the telephone presentation will end in failure.

### 2. The Introduction Should Be Short

A solid introduction should be no more than ten to twenty seconds. Anything longer limits the attention span and availability of the customer, and convolutes the main messages that come after the introduction. Certainly, there will be instances when interaction between the customer and TSR increases that time, so the gauge of ten or twenty seconds is merely a barometer, not set in stone by any means. The key is to keep it short, and not have the introduction become a presentation all its own.

### 3. The Introduction Should Convey A Positive Message

Every customer wishes to hear that a TSR is calling for a positive reason. Clearly, if an introduction is uninviting to the customer, the presentation will fail. A telephone introduction must be dynamic and exciting.

### 4. The Introduction Should Be Forward Thinking

Every introduction must be presented as the beginning of something good for the customer. Hence, the customer has to understand that what he is <u>about to hear</u> is very much worth hearing and will benefit him in the future.

### 5. The Introduction Should Be Polite

When the customer perceives very early within the introduction that the TSR is polite, the customer will have the respect to stay with the telephone presentation longer than if he perceives the TSR is confrontational or selfish.

### 6. The Introduction Should Be Confident

The TSR must believe that every call will result in a completed sale. Confidence is the trait all TSRs must demonstrate in telephone sales.

### 7. The Introduction Must Cover three Points

Who is the TSR?

What does the TSR represent?

What does the TSR want out of the customer?

**TELE-TIP**

When either designing telephone sales scripts, teaching scripting, or formulating a telephone sales game plan, I let TSRs know clearly that all telephone sales scripts can easily be predicated upon seven levels.

The introduction to a telephone sales presentation actually encompasses two sub-levels. The first sub-level introduces the TSR and the company the TSR represents to the customer. This first part of the introduction attempts to establish some sort of rapport or familiarity with the customer.

"Hello Mr. Jones. My name is Larry Darry with XYZ Company. How are you today?"

"Ms. Smith, I was hoping to spend a few minutes with you today. My name is Larry Darry from XYZ Company."

"I'm so excited I was able to reach you at work today. My name is Larry, and I represent XYZ Company. Have you heard of us before?"

The second sub-level introduces the product to the customer. This level attempts to establish credibility, excitement and a desire on the customer's part.

"The reason for my call is to interest you in previewing one of our exciting candle sets."

"The purpose for this call is to spend some time chatting with you about the time shares our company offers to families interested in the island of Cuba."

"I'm calling tonight to chat with you about the exciting world of homeowners' insurance."

By combining the first sub-level of the introduction with the second sub-level of the introduction, the TSR has a solid ten to twenty second introduction to present to his customer.

"Hello Mr. Jones. My name is Larry Darry with XYZ Company. How are you today? The reason for my call is to interest you in previewing one of our exciting candle sets."

"Ms. Smith, I was hoping to spend a few minutes with you today. My name is Larry Darry from XYZ Company. The purpose for this call is to spend some time chatting with you about the time shares our company offers to families interested in seeing Hawaii."

"I'm so excited I was able to reach you at work today. My name is Larry, and I represent XYZ Company. Have you heard of us before? I'm calling tonight to chat with you about the exciting world of homeowners' insurance."

## QUALIFICATION

The qualification of the customer determines whether the TSR should continue on to the next presentation level. Most telephone sales representatives who qualify well know whether they will come away with sales. In contrast, those TSRs who don't qualify well before they enter their presentation levels end up with a minimal amount of sales, *and wonder why.*

I know a fantastic telephone sales representative who qualified so thoroughly prior to presenting the program to customers that he actually let more than 50% of his calls each day hang up without presenting the program. This meant that out of 75 introductions, for example, he would tell nearly 40 of them that they weren't right for his product! His philosophy was simple. He didn't want to waste his time pitching non-qualified customers, and he didn't want non-qualified customers wasting his time, and theirs, asking questions. There is only so much time in a telephone sales shift, and this TSR didn't want to spend his time with customers who couldn't make a positive decision.

**TELE-TIP**

When two different parties meet one another for the first time, there is always an element of friction that develops. To ensure the telephone presentation is successful, this friction must become positive. To do this successfully, the TSR must establish in his telephone introduction seven objectives and utilize those seven objectives completely.

Qualifying customers entails asking questions. In future chapters we are going to learn about probing questions, which are questions the TSR asks to find out pertinent information in order to complete sales. *Qualifying questions are different from probing questions.* Qualifying questions are questions the TSR asks to find out pertinent information in order to discover the following:

Is the customer somebody who can use this product?

Is the customer somebody who can afford this product?

Is the customer somebody who might want this product?

Is the customer somebody who might need this product?

Is the customer somebody who has time to listen to the presentation?

Is the customer somebody who is open to a telephone sales presentation?

Is the customer somebody who can commit over the telephone?

Is the customer somebody to which the TSR wants to present the program?

It is more important that the TSR try to find qualified customers and then present the program to them than it is for the TSR to attempt to squeeze completed sales out of customers who aren't properly qualified. Must the customer meet each of the criteria above? Certainly not. Should the customer meet a few of the criteria above? Absolutely. An old phrase in telephone sales is that "It's a numbers game, so keep dialing". This is true, but it is also "a qualified game, so keep dialing". It isn't enough for a TSR to just find customers; he must find qualified customers. If not, the presentation isn't worth presenting. For example, if the TSR deduces that the customer is not somebody who can use the product, then continuing to present the program will only waste time. (i.e. If the TSR is selling fax machines only to businesses, but the TSR calls a customer at home by mistake, it is foolish for him to continue with the presentation. Likewise, if the TSR deduces that the customer has only five minutes to listen, and the presentation takes fifteen to twenty minutes, then clearly the TSR shouldn't present the program at that moment but instead should call back another day.)

The importance of qualifying thoroughly prior to beginning a presentation is clear. TSRs must be willing to ask the right questions in order to find out if the customer is worth presenting the program to, and they must learn *how* to ask those questions prior to beginning a presentation.

## THE CONCEPT OF QUALIFYING QUESTIONS

Too often I have monitored good TSRs who asked solid qualifying questions, but then didn't understand what to do with the answers after the customer responded. This is a great example of a TSR who doesn't understand *how* the concept of asking qualifying questions can make all of the difference in the world. They were taught, correctly, that qualifying questions gave them answers that could provide them with information. They were not taught, however, that every question asked has a particular style and element to it, and that the questions asked mean something to the overall sales presentation. To resolve this dilemma, I have created five questions a TSR should be able to ask of himself and answer *prior* to making a telephone sales presentation and entering the qualification stages of that call:

**Most telephone sales representatives who qualify well know whether they will come away with sales. In contrast, those TSRs who don't qualify well before they enter their presentation levels end up with a minimal amount of sales.**

1.  **Which questions must the TSR ask of which customers?**

    All customers are not the same, and this means that all customers shouldn't be treated as if they were the same. Simple set-up qualifying questions such as "Have you heard of our product before?" or "Do you own a Toyota?" may not have to be asked if the TSR has the answers, or if the questions aren't applicable.

2.  **How many questions should the TSR ask of each customer?**

    Some customers respond much better to questions than others. Therefore, every customer, depending on the situation, should be asked a different number of qualifying questions.

3.  **What do the customer's responses mean to the telephone presentation?**

    This is the most important thing the TSR must learn. Asking questions is useless if the answers don't mean anything, and the downfall of many TSRs is that the answers they receive usually <u>don't</u> mean anything to them. Utilizing the listening and hearing skills we learned in previous chapters, the TSR must learn to grasp the content of the customer's answer and then use it to his advantage.

4.  **In what style should each question be presented?**

    Depending on the customer, the style of each question is very important. Every customer, as we explored earlier, responds to a different tone, pace, melody and inflection. In addition, some customers respond better to questions when they are asked in an urgent setting, while others provide better answers in a relaxed setting. Part of qualifying a customer correctly is to understand what the customer's needs are prior to beginning the question and answer process. Perhaps the customer would have provided tremendous answers if only he or she had received a verbal smile prior to the TSR asking the qualifying questions.

5.  **How important is the "time factor" when qualifying the customer?**

    This is very critical for the TSR to understand. If a customer states that he has only ten minutes to talk, qualifying this customer can't take eight minutes, because there will be little time left for the actual telephone sales presentation. In such an instance, perhaps the TSR should call the customer back at a time that is more convenient for him. Or, if ten minutes is enough time to present the program, the TSR then has to understand what percentage of the ten minutes should be spent in qualifying.

## BEST WORDS WHEN ESTABLISHING A QUALIFYING QUESTION OVER THE TELEPHONE

May I

Will

Is

Let me

How

Where

What

"May I ask, how often have you looked into joining other plans?"

"Will there be an opportunity to meet with you before you go on vacation?"

"Is your wife somebody who enjoys fishing?"

"Let me ask you, what are some of the foods you eat on weekends?"

"How do you go about making reservations when you travel overseas?"

"Where did you and your son sit when you attended the baseball game last April?"

"What are two or three ideas you have for creating better posters?"

## SIX TECHNIQUES FOR APPROACHING A QUALIFYING QUESTION

1. **Find the Right Time**

   It is so easy to ask a customer a question at the wrong time. If the customer has something to say, don't interrupt his flow by asking a question. If the TSR is still developing rapport with the customer, asking questions is the wrong approach, as the TSR may come off as too aggressive and scare the customer away.

2. **Begin with a Transition Phrase**

   Have you ever had a conversation with somebody who kept shooting questions at you? It gets pretty irritating, because the questions come quickly. When asking a question, it's important to lead into the question, as opposed to asking it outright. Take this paragraph for example. I could have started this paragraph with:

> "When asking a question, it's important to lead into the question, as opposed to asking it outright."

Instead, I began it with this transition:

> "Have you ever had a conversation with somebody who kept shooting questions at you? It gets pretty irritating, because the questions come quickly."

## 3. Don't Stumble

By asking a question, the TSR is giving the customer an opportunity to play "equal" with him in the sales conversation. Certainly, the customer will provide information, but the customer may give the TSR information that he may not be prepared to handle. So if the TSR and his customer are now equals, it is mandatory that every question comes off as secure. Stumbling over the phone represents either confusion or insincerity, both of which the customer will sense quickly.

## 4. Use Inflection, Pace and Tone Appropriately

The words a TSR uses in a question are important, but the way he actually asks that question is even more important. Below are five examples of how one phrase can be turned around.

Did you go to jail?

Did **you** go to jail?

Did you go to **jail**?

**Did** you go to jail?

Did you **go** to jail?

## 5. Ask Direct Questions

Customers don't want to be patronized and they don't want to be played with. Thus, when asking a question, just ask it. Don't beat around the bush, because that sounds threatening. Also, if the TSR needs to know an answer, it is important to get that answer succinctly. So, ask succinct questions.

## 6. Converse Between Questions

This is where trust becomes so important. I mentioned earlier that shooting one question after another does no good for a customer without some sort of human interaction. Break up questions with comments and points of interest, even if those comments and points of interest don't help to validate the TSR's presentation.

**CHILDREN'S BOOKS SELLING EXAMPLE**

*Because questions are designed to illicit responses which the TSR can use, the TSR should decide prior to making a telephone sales call which questions he believes would most benefit him in making the sale, and what answers he would like to hear in the optimum scenario. For example, if the TSR believes the following questions would help him complete a children's books sale, then the TSR should ask these questions first in order to get the best idea of what his customer needs.*

"Do you have children who read children's books?"

"May I ask, what mystery book writers most appeal to you?"

"How old are your children?"

"Let me ask you, how many books do you purchase in a year?"

"Have you ever purchased books of any kind over the telephone?"

"Will you allow me 10 minutes to tell you a bit about our program?"

"What are some of the Dr. Seuss books that your children enjoy?"

"Where are the bookstores and libraries nearest to your house?"

## THREE "MUST" QUALIFYING QUESTIONS FOR EVERY TELEPHONE PRESENTATION

When qualifying a customer over the telephone, there are three questions all TSRs must ask and which need to be answered in nearly 99% of all telephone sales presentations. Even when TSRs understand what they must ask and what answers they are looking for, asking these three questions will always give the TSR a good idea of exactly what is needed to sell within the presentation and close the sale:

"Mr. Smith, what do you presently have now?"

"Ms. Jones, what are some of your thoughts on the products and services you presently have?"

"Mr. Smith, who are the decision makers, besides yourself?"

The golden rules when qualifying a customer are clear: the TSR must make each and every qualifying question matter for both the TSR and the customer, and the TSR must understand why each qualifying question matters for both himself and his customer.

## OBTAINING A CUSTOMER'S FULL ATTENTION

"Hello? Have you heard a word I'm saying?"

That's a question TSRs want to ask their customers when they feel they aren't making progress, but because of the TSRs' need to maintain professionalism, they can't. It is quite common for the TSR to feel as if the customer has drifted off into another land. And, in many instances, the customer <u>has</u> drifted off into another land!!! This may be for any number of reasons, but the reasons are not nearly as important as what happens to the sales presentation when the customer drifts off. When customers don't pay attention, sales don't get made. <u>Customers will never make buying decisions or any other decisions over the telephone without first making sure that the investment they are about to make is worthwhile</u>. Hence, gaining and maintaining a customer's full attention throughout a presentation is absolutely mandatory for success, if for no other reason than the customer will demand, prior to completing the sale, that he has every ounce of information he needs. ("Well, if you were listening the last 20 minutes, you would have heard everything the first time!")

I believe that gaining and maintaining a customer's attention over the telephone is far more difficult than gaining and maintaining a customer's attention in person. In person, the sales representative can use all sorts of exterior aspects to coordinate attention, such as props, the hand, eye contact, and movement. The sales representative can easily see when the customer is becoming distracted. Over the telephone, the TSR doesn't have these advantages, but he does have advantages he can use when selling over the telephone.

**TELE-TIP**

Every question asked has a particular style and element to it, and the questions asked mean something to the overall sales presentation.

Here are six ways for a TSR to establish a customer's full attention:

1. **Confirm with customers prior to the presentation that they are available and willing to communicate**

   Prior to the actual presentation, it is mandatory that the TSR confirm with the customer that he has the time and willingness to chat. A simple qualifying question and a commitment on the customer's part is all that is needed.

   "Is now a good time to talk?"

   "Can I tell you a bit about our program?"

   "Do you have a few minutes, or is it better that we chat later?"

2. **Get customers involved in the conversation by making sure they provide comments**

   This keeps them mentally aware of what the TSR is saying and provides the TSR with the necessary information to make the presentation better. Ask them questions such as:

   "What are your thoughts on that?"

   "Do you agree with me?"

   "How would you go about that?"

3. **Make the presentation sound interesting enough that it is worthwhile for the customers to listen**

   We are all in agreement that a dull, monotone presentation is boring for the customer and will not spur the customer to be excited about making decisions over the telephone. The telephone sales representative's goal is to use his voice to excite the customers, soothe the customers or force the customers to act. The analogy I like to use is that the TSR must, while on the telephone, pretend he is on the radio. If the TSR were a disc jockey, he would understand that when people listen to the radio they listen to different stations to receive different types of stimulation. The choice is theirs, as it is the customer's choice to listen to the TSR. When people listen to the news stations, they are looking for knowledge, and tend to pay attention to the bits or pieces that sound informative. When people listen to the talk radio stations they are listening for general stimulation, but they also tend to stop listening quickly if the subject is of little interest. Talk radio disc jockeys have high voice patterns, balancing inflection with humor, based on the topic of conversation. Making a presentation sound interesting can be approached in two ways: the words the TSR uses and the style in which he presents those words. Style is the more important of the two.

4. **Make sure customers are not only listening to what the TSR is saying but hearing what the TSR is saying**

   Ask the customers questions throughout the presentation that invite decision-making responses. If the TSR hears customers give verbal nods, then he knows they are practicing their listening skills. But unless the TSR asks them questions that allow them to answer him with an element of depth, the TSR won't be sure that they are hearing and understanding what is being said. Examples of such questions include:

   "Would you favor…?"

   "Would low cost programs interest you more for today or for the future?"

   "What types of products do you use in your business every day?"

   "If you could improve your business in any way, what would it be?"

   "What can I say that will make you more interested?"

5. **Provide excitement and opportunity to upcoming parts of the presentation**

Stand-up comedians and movie theaters have mastered the art of promoting upcoming events to both gain and maintain the customers' interest. Headline comedians have a "warm-up" act to motivate the audience for the main act. Sometimes the warm-up act is so funny that the audience can't wait to hear the main show. Other times, the warm-up act is so poor that the audience also can't wait to get him off stage because the main act will have to be better! Movie previews provide the same anticipation. After three or four

*Gaining and maintaining a customer's full attention throughout a presentation is absolutely mandatory for success, if for no other reason than the customer will demand, prior to completing the sale, that he has every ounce of information he needs.*

extremely good movie previews, the audience is usually buzzing when the main feature begins, and that adds adrenaline for the show. The TSR should incorporate these traits into his presentation, also promoting what the customer can learn if he maintains his attention. The following lines work best:

"Mr. Jones, if you think that sounds good, let me tell you about this."

"Ms. Smith, I haven't even gotten to the best part yet."

"I want to tell you the price first. Then, I'll let you know
what that includes."

"If you think that's good, wait until I get to the bonus plan as well."

### 6. Be creative with the presentation

TSRs all too often communicate over the phone as if they are straight, stiff men in a bad drama. This is caused by inexperience, and also leads to stereotyping. There is no reason for the telephone sales representative to play the part of the serious, somber, dramatic sales person. Customers like humans, and they like creative humans who incorporate comedy, self-deprecation and reality into a presentation. It is okay for the TSR to stray from the main goal if the TSR can control the stray and bring the conversation back at any time. In addition, good TSRs can let the customer dominate the conversation as long as the TSR can get it back. This creativity adds dynamite to the life of a telephone sales presentation.

In the following chapters, we continue to focus on the concept of the presentation level as the focal point toward selling over the telephone. This chapter studied the theory of presentation levels, the introduction and qualification of a presentation, and the techniques for obtaining the customer's full attention during the presentation. The next chapter deals with the next step in the cycle: staying focused on the direction of the telephone sales presentation.

# CHAPTER 5

## DIRECTING THE SALES PRESENTATION

Imagine for a moment that you aren't preparing to be an exceptional TSR. Instead, you are a race car driver on a 100 mile race through one of the largest and most complicated cities in the world!!! Your goal is to manipulate the road with one primary objective in mind: to win the race. Manipulating the road means you take the twists, turns, off-ramps and on-ramps with a certain confidence and with dynamic control. Your turns are sharp, the wheels are literally floating above the road. You know your competition exists, because when the race began you were all together. But now, they are out of sight and out of mind. You are in the groove, focusing, maintaining strict control over your race car, dodging road debris. Your mind is ahead of the race as you reach the halfway point. You are thinking ahead, preparing for turnoffs and stops, gauging your gas, analyzing your speed. Your car is humming along, your hands are fire on the steering wheel. Shifting has never been so easy, and race car driving has never been so much fun. You are staying focused on the direction of your race.

Although the reality of our world dictates that we are not race car drivers, the analogy between race car driving and telephone selling is quite appropriate when looking at the life of a TSR. The TSR's job, like the race car driver's, is to handle the telephone call like a world class speedster handles the road. In looking at the traits we mentioned above and breaking them down, the TSR will see how the analogies stack up. The TSR is the race car driver. His goal is to manipulate the telephone call with one primary objective: to close the sale. *He is the person* who starts the engine, who announces to the customer that he is ready to drive, who moves the telephone call onto the highway. *He is the person* who must keep himself, the car and the road focused on the direction of his race.

As we explore telephone selling, we will learn that many of the fundamentals a TSR applies throughout the presentation are of very little importance if he cannot establish and sustain control over the direction of the call from its very inception. All too often, TSRs fail to truly recognize that maintaining the direction of the telephone call is the most important fundamental of them all!

Obviously, there are a variety of reasons why maintaining the direction of the telephone call is so fundamental to telephone sales. *First*, customers are going to attempt to take the telephone presentation all over the place. There will never be a period in a telephone call when a customer isn't going to be dodging questions in order to ask his own, or asking questions the TSR is completely unprepared to answer. Customers tend not to know where they want to go with the conversation, and this, of course, can be very dangerous. If customers knew where they wanted to go, then a simple focus of the call between customer and TSR would be established. They don't. Customers are like drunk drivers, swerving their comments and thoughts and answers and decisions all over the place. The reason why it is so scary being on the road with a drunk driver is not that the driver is drunk but that he can't stay in his own lane, he doesn't obey the laws, he is indecisive and incoherent, he ignores traffic lights and signs, and he doesn't really have any feelings or sympathy for anybody else on the road. In that same respect customers are scary and a hazard to TSRs. Customers will always try to take control of the presentation, and this means that the TSR will always find it challenging to accomplish anything. *Second,* TSRs have a tendency to relinquish control of a call when the customer takes control, because customers who attempt to take control of presentations are far more confident than TSRs who try to take it back. Customers take control by asking questions, making statements and appearing to be decisive about their decisions. On the face of it, this would appear to be positive, because with such consistency by customers, one would think the TSR would know exactly what is going on. Yet, there is little advantage in this situation for the TSR, because the minute a TSR gives up control, the TSR will never be able to recapture control. For example, if the TSR wants to sell a certain aspect of children's books (i.e. low prices), and the customer continues to question the TSR about the quality of the stories, the TSR will never be able to sell the aspect of the children's books that he wants to sell, because the customer won't let him. Who has control? The customer. *Third,* maintaining direction of the presentation not only increases the percentages that a sale will be completed, but it also allows the TSR to do his very best in meeting the primary objectives of his telephone call. There is nothing more frustrating than making a telephone call to a qualified prospect and not having the opportunity to walk away from the call with a completed sale, or completed objectives. Why talk on the telephone if the telephone sales representative doesn't have any control over the call? Objectives are why TSRs call customers.

Within each sales presentation, the TSR must have a solid, primary objective in mind. This objective is normally provided by the company he is working for, and in most instances this primary objective involves gaining commitment from the customer (i.e., commitment to buy something, commitment to meet somebody, commitment to preview something). In every area of telephone sales, there must be a primary objective.

It is important that the focus on the TSR's primary objective stays the same. This is most difficult for TSRs. I have monitored calls that go on and on and on with no end until the <u>customer</u> (not the TSR) finally initiates a close to the call. The primary objective was communicated from the TSR to the customer, but as the call went forth the objective was ignored and different subjects were talked about. What happened to the sales person? The TSR remembered what his primary objective was at the beginning of his call, forgot what his primary objective was as he got wrapped up in the call, and missed out on making a sale.

### THE CHILDREN'S BOOKS SELLING EXAMPLE

*The primary objective when selling this product is to get the customer to purchase a set of six children's books for $29.99.*

The primary objective of the above telephone sell is clear. Anything less than completing a sale with each customer would be less than the primary objective.

There are, however, in almost all telephone sales presentations, secondary objectives, and most often there are many secondary objectives to a sales call. Why should the TSR trap himself into selling one objective if that objective simply can't be met? In a case like that, it is imperative for the TSR to diverge away from the primary objective and meet one of the secondary objectives.

### THE CHILDREN'S BOOKS SELLING EXAMPLE

*A secondary objective when selling this product is to get the customer to preview a set of the children's books. Another secondary objective would be to get the customer to accept information about the children's books. Still another secondary objective would be to get the customer to agree to preview one of the six children's books, and, if applicable, order the other five books at another time.*

Good products have many different objectives and options for the TSR to utilize throughout the presentation. The TSR isn't trapped into making decisions on behalf of his customers when these decisions may not be the very best ones available. He has a plethora of options, directions and avenues to explore in the presentation in order to make a success out of it.

## HOW TO ESTABLISH THE DIRECTION OF A CALL

The *first step* in establishing the direction of a call is to do so within the first two minutes, because the first two minutes of a telephone sales call will establish the direction of that call in 85% of all cases. In the first two minutes, the TSR sets the foundation by introducing himself, asking questions of the customer, and explaining the primary objective of the call. If the TSR is confident and in command of his facts, he will likely sustain a high ratio of success in qualifying the customer appropriately and, if applicable, moving the conversation on to the next level. Also, if the TSR is confident and in command of his facts, he will have a much better chance of sustaining control of the telephone call long term. When it comes to maintaining direction of the presentation, recognizing when the call is lost is key. Because control of a call is gained in the first two minutes, it is a good bet the direction was lost there. Hence, to ensure the TSR will retain direction of the call, the *second step* is to make sure the TSR has complete knowledge of his product available, and is entirely confident of his position from the beginning.

---

### THE CHILDREN'S BOOKS SELLING EXAMPLE

*Below is an example of what happens when a TSR is not confident of his position and/or knowledgeable about his product, during the first 2 minutes.*

TSR "Mr. Smith, I would like to talk to you about these fantastic children's books."

MR. SMITH "Before you do, I have a few questions to ask you. Can you tell me who publishes the books, who writes the books and who the artist is who drew the pictures?"

TSR "That is a good question, but I don't have an answer for you right now. If you would like to hold on for a moment, I think I can find out for you, after I tell you a bit about how fantastic these children's books are."

MR. SMITH "It is more important to me that I find out what I need to know. Please give me a call back when you can find out the information. Thank you."

---

In the above example, which occurs with alarmingly high frequency, we can see how the TSR <u>intended</u> to establish the direction of the presentation, but was thrown for a loop when the customer took that direction away from him. It is good that the TSR tried to establish direction, but he wasn't prepared enough or confident enough to do so. The TSR began the process with a clear objective: to talk to the customer about how fantastic his children's books are. Unfortunately, the TSR was unable to establish direction, and his lack of preparation showed through greatly when the customer threw him for a loop.

The TSR must remember the points we reviewed previously – that customers never go in the direction the TSR wants them to go in, and that exceptional knowledge of the product will allow the TSR to be fast enough and versatile enough to compensate for this. There is no reason why the above sample call couldn't have turned into a completed sale for the TSR! The only reason why it didn't was that the TSR was unprepared, and wasn't adaptable when it came time to be so.

---

### THE CHILDREN'S BOOKS SELLING EXAMPLE

*Below is an example of what happens when a TSR is confident of his position and knowledgeable about his product during the first two minutes of a call. Note the flexibility the TSR displays in putting this call back on track.*

TSR   "Mr. Smith, I would like to talk to you about these fantastic children's books."

MR. SMITH "Before you do, I have a few questions to ask you. Can you tell me who makes the books, who writes the books and who the artist is who drew the pictures for the books?"

TSR   "That is a good question, and I'd be happy to answer it, because that ties in directly to what I was hoping to chat with you about. Our children's books are fantastic for your child because of the three very reasons you mentioned. The books are made by the X company, written by the Y author, and pictures for the book were illustrated by the Z artist. Are you familiar with them?"

---

Flexible TSRs can adapt when needed, and recover strongly to complete a sale. Product knowledge and confidence play a huge role in establishing this adaptability.

The *third step* in establishing the direction of a call is to ensure that the TSR communicates to the customer exactly where he wants that call to go. A large reason why telephone calls don't go in the TSR's favor is because the TSR hasn't successfully communicated which way the call should go. Customers sit, phone in hand, waiting to find out exactly what kind of conversation they are getting themselves into. All the while, the TSR drones on

Customers never go in the direction the TSR wants them to go in, and exceptional knowledge of the product will allow the TSR to be fast enough and versatile enough to compensate for this.

and on about inconsequential items that have little or no impact on the primary objective of the telephone sales presentation. Or, even worse, the TSR drones on and on about items in which the customer has no interest, thus losing the customer quickly. The TSR must communicate succinctly what he is trying to accomplish! This ties in to a simple preparation game that sportscasters and newscasters practice all of the time. What is good for sportscasters and newscasters is good for telephone sales reps as well.

Sportscasters and newscasters always arrive to work early. Baseball sportscasters get to the ballpark as much as four hours before the game. Newscasters do the same, arriving even earlier to the studio, because they need to prepare their newscast. Prior to the start of a ballgame, sportscasters sit in the broadcast booth and practice the opening segment of their broadcast over and over again. Finally, when we hear the beginning broadcast, we are listening to hours of well thought out and rehearsed words. Newscasters practice the same way as do sportscasters. Prior to the beginning of a newscast, the first few stories are rehearsed completely. Perhaps the rest of the broadcast is either semi-known or read cold, but the first few stories are practiced to enhance fluidity. Both sportscasters and newscasters know exactly where they want their presentations to go!!

I believe that at least ten minutes prior to the start of a telephone sales shift, the TSR should be in his seat preparing his opening presentation. More importantly, the TSR should be practicing his opening presentation as it relates to maintaining direction of the conversation. The TSR should practice his calls by stating sample objections out loud, and then providing the rebuttals that will maintain the direction of the call. Practice, Practice, Practice!

The *fourth step* in gaining direction of a telephone call is perhaps the most people-oriented step of the group. Making the customers comprehend that you are interested in them is a quality and people oriented step to gaining direction of a telephone call. Have you ever been on a date, or on the phone with friends, and found that there was no progress being made because the person on the other end didn't really seem to be involved? Let's face it, it happens to even the best of us. Perhaps you are at work and you are trying to communicate an important concept to your boss, and you are getting little or no results. He isn't paying attention. Perhaps you are talking to your wife or husband, and you know, deep down inside, that they just aren't listening. The disappointment we all register in those situations is palatable. We as individuals want others to pay attention to us. Making the customer comprehend that you are interested in him is an important step toward gaining direction of a telephone sales presentation. Customers will give up direction of a sales call to the TSR if they feel they have an honest reason for giving it up, and if they have a high comfort level in doing so. They should not be made to feel as if they are being coerced to listen to a telephone call, nor should they be made to feel as if they are being left out of the conversation. Customers should feel as if they are equal partners in the conversation, and if they have that comfort level, then the telephone sales representative's ability to maintain direction of the call becomes much simpler.

**TELE-TIP**

If the TSR is confident and in command of his facts, he will likely find a high ratio of success in qualifying the customer appropriately and, if applicable, moving the conversation on to the next level. Also, if the TSR is confident and in command of his facts, he will have a much better chance of sustaining control of the telephone call long term.

Asking questions motivates the customer to become involved in the presentation. The more questions a TSR asks, the more involved the customer becomes, and soon the TSR is leading the call in exactly the direction he wants it to go. In addition, small one liners become very important in this situation as well.

"It's very important to me we find out......"

"I feel strongly this will help......"

"The goal of our company is to make you and your family......"

"What's important is that you take your time......"

The *fifth and final step* toward maintaining direction of a telephone call is to ensure, at all times, that the call is moving <u>forward</u>. This step combines principles from the other four steps along with previously discussed traits:

Flexibility

Adaptability

Creativity

Focus

Rapport

Practice

"Keep that ball moving" is an old basketball-coaching axiom. The basketball in a basketball game must always be moving, so the game establishes a consistent flow. When the ball is moving, the team with the ball always has complete control, and they have a much greater percentage opportunity to place the ball through the basket, completing their primary objective. In <u>telephone selling, keeping the presentation moving forward is just as important as keeping the ball moving in basketball</u>. Even if the conversation is entertaining and the subject is valuable, the customer has to feel that there is an end objective to the telephone call.

If a conversation is very humorous, that means there is a comfort level between the TSR and the customer. But when does that humor begin to overshadow the TSR's ability to complete the sale? I have often counseled TSR's who enjoy certain conversation pieces so much that they never move the conversation past a friendly chat-in-the-park.

The TSR can keep the telephone presentation moving forward by understanding what he needs at every point along the way. For example, if a conversation is very humorous, that means there is a comfort level between the TSR and the customer. But when does that humor begin to overshadow the TSR's ability to complete the sale? I have often counseled TSRs who enjoy certain conversation pieces so much that they never move the conversation past a friendly chat-in-the-park. Subjects need to be explored but the call needs to be kept moving forward, or staleness will ensue.

### MAINTAINING DIRECTION OF THE CALL

With so many new sales channels opening up in this age of technology, the art of maintaining direction over the telephone becomes that much more challenging. None of us were alive when the telephone was first developed, and very few of us were alive when telephone selling first began, somewhere around the first quarter of the 20th century. To my knowledge, no documents on how to sell over the telephone existed at that time. Yet telephone selling existed on a small scale, and as the years went by it proliferated. I can bet this much. During those first telephone sales calls in the early 20th century, TSRs had their customers' rapt attention! Gaining direction of the call wasn't a sales technique that needed to be studied because every presentation had the customer's direct attention. Short of door-to-door service, (which was very popular) sales makers didn't come to the home. Telephone calling was unique, interesting, different, and I am sure each TSR was able to communicate everything he needed to. However, a century later, things have changed quite a bit. Selling in the home has proliferated with targeted door-to-door service, direct mail, telephone selling, the Internet, television shopping channels and television and radio commercials. With that proliferation comes enhanced customer knowledge, and that means, in some cases, enhanced customer annoyance. Customers today don't let TSRs maintain easy direction of telephone calls simply because the Internet and television shopping channels allow a simpler manner of purchase, *with the customer retaining complete control.* If the customer doesn't want to listen, he uses the remote control and turns the program off. It is a lot easier for the customer to maintain direction of the sale by turning off the television than it is to be rude to a human being on the other end of the telephone line, all of which leads to the fact that with increased sales opportunities, maintaining direction of the telephone presentation is that much more difficult.

Below are eight skill-sets a TSR must utilize before, during, and after a telephone sales presentation in order to stay focused on ensuring direction of the call.

1. **Command Direction**

    If the TSR is not in command of the call, the customer will take the conversation to places the telephone sales rep isn't prepared to go, and the sales presentation will fail.

2. **Understand Pace**

    The TSR must let the customer establish the actual pace of the call, such as speed and dialect. Then the TSR must match his delivery to his customer's in order to gain good rapport and trust.

3. **Direct the Primary Goal**

    Often customers and telephone sales reps go off on tangents, discussing everything except the primary goal of the call. Every telephone sales rep must remain focused on not getting too comfortable himself lest he forget the primary goal.

4. **Move To Secondary Objectives**

    Sometimes the primary goal just isn't reachable. A sudden shift in conversation, style or topic can throw an entire presentation off of the primary goal. In that case, the presentation needs to be rescued by transitioning to the first of the secondary objectives.

5. **Don't Lose Control**

    Experience will help the telephone sales representative learn when a conversation has gone too far. Always remember that the TSR must first <u>establish</u> direction and then <u>maintain</u> direction to complete the sale.

6.  **Learn Skills**

By studying this book and many others like it, the TSR will acquire the skills to maintain direction. Then, the TSR must continually practice, read trade journals, and monitor peers.

7.  **Understand Percentages, Hours, And Goals**

<u>When it comes to percentages</u>, I go by the 90-10 rejection rule. In almost all telemarketing assignments that involve sales or direct persuasion over the telephone, 90% of the time the customer will refuse the sale no matter what tactics are utilized, and the TSR will have to move on to the next call. Thus, no matter who plays the part of the sales person, 90% of all calls will be refusals.

**TELE-TIP**

Telephone selling is a lot like baseball. The more the TSR practices and performs, the more the TSR succeeds.

Obviously, this number is epic in proportion, and the percentage of people who decline telephone sales offers is one of the difficult aspects of this job.

<u>When it comes to hours</u>, the TSR must be aware that a job requires him to fulfill a certain period of time, so he must fulfill that time regardless of his passion or lack of passion for the position. When I managed telephone sales reps whom were required to work only eighteen hours per week, many couldn't because of conflicts or other reasons. Certainly they were not expected to be as committed to part-time jobs as they might have been to full-time jobs, but they still were compelled to put in the agreed upon hours, for two basic reasons. First, because the hours they had committed to were guaranteed, and their employer was counting on them to work these hours. The employer had budgeted hours accordingly, and expected the TSRs to fulfill their promises. Showing up late consistently plays against a TSR's chances of doing well, and missing days without making up the agreed upon hours sets both TSR and employer back. Second, because telephone selling is a lot like baseball, the more the TSR practices and performs, the more the TSR succeeds. No TSR can make money without working, and no telemarketer can make great money and become a success without practicing the craft over and over again. When committing to a job, the TSR must make sure the hours are comfortable and easy to maintain.

<u>When it comes to goals</u>, the TSR must realize that when working in any business there must be a minimum standard required to maintain employment. Even the friendliest job with the most relaxed and upstanding atmosphere requires goals. At one of my jobs, when managing full-time telephone sales reps, I required that my TSRs accomplish a minimum of eleven contacts per hour to maintain a seat on the floor. I made sure to explain the requirement and the review process to each employee throughout the employment interview, so that when it came time to assess achievement, I knew the employees and I were on the same page. Not all managers will set forth the goals so clearly at the initial interview. Thus, it is up

to the telephone sales representative to ask the right questions so he will know exactly what the job requires.

## 8. Take Time To Gain Knowledge

John Wooden, the former UCLA basketball coach, has a wonderful saying:

"Failing to prepare is preparing to fail."

The direction of a telephone call can't be maintained if the TSR fails to prepare.

## MAINTAINING DIRECTION OF A CALL WHEN THE CUSTOMER SWINGS ELSEWHERE

The fun and challenging part of maintaining direction of a telephone call does not take place when the customer gives up control to the TSR, but when the customer seems to be on his own agenda, and won't let the TSR get the call back on track. This is where the competition between customer and TSR becomes a fascinating example of telephone selling. When this scenario comes into play, there is a bit of "one-on-one" sportsmanship involved. Who will capture the direction of the call?

Again, an everyday analogy is in order. I hope no reader ever finds himself in this situation, but it is appropriate. Imagine that an individual is driving down a winding road, and the steering wheel begins to fail to respond to his actions. At first, the steering wheel needs to be tugged a little more sharply to the left or right in order to enhance movement of the car. But then things get progressively worse. Finally, the steering wheel doesn't respond on one turn until the last second, and the car seems to have a mind of its own. What does one do?

I have no idea.

But I do know how one controls an out of control customer, a customer who, after receiving a telephone call, decides to go his own way. The primary step in handling this is to understand exactly what paths the customer traveled *prior* to the telephone call taking place, and then understand exactly *which* paths the TSR can take in order to get the conversation back on track.

There are primarily two difficult paths customers take even though TSRs don't want them to. These are the paths that TSRs cringe over when they hear customers going that route. I call them the "No, don't go there" paths that TSRs must understand how to overcome. The two paths customers always want to take during telephone sales calls are the one about price, and the other about the legitimacy of the item they are considering buying. No matter how hard the TSR works to swing the conversation back toward the items he wishes to talk about, all customers really care about in the end is how much the product is going to cost them, and how legitimate the product is for the customer or the customer's family. I am a strong believer, however, that as long as the TSR is prepared to handle a customer who is demanding to know about the price and legitimacy of the product, the TSR will be able to regain direction of the presentation a majority of the time.

---

### THE CHILDREN'S BOOKS SELLING EXAMPLE
*Failing to overcome the price barrier*

TSR: "I have a great item I know you are going to enjoy."

CUSTOMER: "That's all well and good, but tell me how much it's going to cost me."

TSR: "I'd like to give you an idea what it's all about so you can see how affordable it really is."

CUSTOMER: "Of course you would like to do that, but I want to know how much it costs before I hear all about it."

---

The above scenario demonstrates the dilemma for an outstanding TSR. The customer was set on maintaining direction of the telephone call, and his stubbornness backed the TSR into a corner. The TSR was obligated to handle the price issue, or everything he said from that time on would not matter to the customer.

The price issue is an issue that truly defeats TSRs. Society has conditioned people to think price first, and to react negatively ("That's too expensive") without thinking things through. Let's recognize one fact clearly. Customers want to talk price first because price scares them more than anything else. With this in mind, TSRs must resist talking about price until they have set the stage and established credibility to support that price. Price is the big deterrent in every sales situation, and even more so when the customer can't see the product being sold to him. Thus, a customer's interest in knowing price first is a subliminal reaction to reassure himself that the product might be worthwhile. Or it is a direct reaction by the customer to find out if staying on the phone might be worthwhile. When dealing with a customer who is focused on the price issue, the TSR must attempt a few statements and questions to swing the customer back to the TSR's objective of the call.

"Mr. Jones, do you agree it is important to learn as much about our offer as you can?"

"Mr. Jones, I very much want to talk about how much it costs, but I don't want to rush you into a decision, and I don't think we are at that stage yet."

"That's a great question, and it is important that I answer it fairly. Can I share a couple things about the product first?"

"I'd be happy to chat about the price with you. Let me ask you a few questions."

"Price is important, I agree. How much are you looking to spend on our product?"

"That's a good question, because everybody I talk with wants to know about price. How come every person I talk to brings up the price issue?"

"Price is a valid concern, and in order to tell you how much it costs, I am going to have to find out some information."

By delivering these statements and questions, the TSR is attempting to convey to the customer how important it is to hear <u>more about the program</u> before tackling the price issue. Also, the TSR is trying to involve the customer in the conversation so the customer begins to lose control of the direction of the call. For example, if the customer says "I want to know about price", then the customer has control over the direction of the call. But if the TSR says "Let me ask you a few questions" or "Can I share a couple of things about the product first?" the TSR is taking control of the call back. Often, just saying "You don't want to talk about price just yet" <u>won't work</u>, because indeed, the customer does want to talk about price, right now!! Asking the customer questions that segue into other subjects, however, allows the conversation to slowly creep back in the direction the TSR is looking to go.

The advantage the TSR has in his efforts to regain control of the telephone presentation is that the TSR understands that direction of the presentation is extremely important. The customer has no idea about direction of telephone calls and maintaining control of conversations. Customers just talk, while maintaining direction is a component of telephone selling at which the TSR makes an effort to succeed . The customer will never think this way. The customer cares about himself, and, thinking linearly, the customer is only thinking price, price, price. This is where a little creativity and adaptability makes all the difference in the world.

**TELE-TIP**

The two paths customers always want to take during telephone sales calls are the path about price, and the path about the legitimacy of the item they are considering buying.

The TSR must also recognize that price is not a barrier when it is stacked up to perceived value. As a telephone sales trainer who has attended many seminars around the country, I am the first one to admit the phrase "perceived value" is overused. How many times can I recall sales trainers who exclaim "Just take price and legitimize that price to perceived value, and everything will be fine."

Too many.

However, the reality of telephone selling is that comparing price to value does work. If the prospect feels comfortable enough in believing that the price of the product is fair in relation to the value the product provides, the TSR has a powerful chance of closing the sale. If, on the other hand, the customer feels the price of the product is completely unfair in relation to the value the product provides, price will become a detriment the TSR can't overcome.

In comparing price to perceived value, the TSR must take his time in framing the debate. There is no need for the TSR to hope the customer will believe that price is equivalent to value. Instead, the TSR must ask questions and sell appropriate benefits and features that will establish price as a credible element to the value of the product.

● **Find Out What The Customer Believes Is Credible About The Product**

Guessing games don't work. Instead, the TSR must ask the customer what he believes is credible about the product, and then put those things in one corner.

"Which areas that we have talked about are you interested in?"

● **Frame the Presentation Around What Those Credible Areas Are Worth**

Once three or four features of a product are deemed credible by the customer, the TSR needs to relate a price and value to those features. For example, if a customer states that good literature, pictures and long lasting durability is what makes him interested in children's books, the TSR has to find out from the customer what he would pay (price) to own books that have those established benefits. Then, the TSR must relate the price the customer states to the value of the books. If the customer states that he would pay less money than the books are being sold for, the TSR can then sell the additional benefits of the program in order to establish credibility with the customer.

"Mr. Smith, you said you would pay $25 for the books as they are.
If I throw in this and that, don't you think the books
would then be worth $50.00?"

"Ms. Jones, you stated that you would pay $75.00 for the books.
Well, they are presently only $50.00. Can you see the value?"

● **Sell the Quality**

Even when customers agree that a product is worth its price, oftentimes they still don't make the decision to purchase. This can become very frustrating for the TSR. On one hand, the TSR has established the price and tied in the credibility of the product to the price. What does the TSR do now? The TSR needs to create a bond between the price and the quality. Customers never want to overpay, and they always want to feel that they received a wonderful deal. By selling quality, customers are going to be able to see much more clearly the correlation between product and price.

Sell the quality of the product versus similar products sold over the phone or in stores.

Sell the quality of the product versus similar products that the customer presently owns.

Sell the quality of the product as it stands on its own.

Sell the quality of the product as it relates to the individual customer.

● **Sell What the Benefits Mean**

Price tends to be less daunting when the benefits stand out. Too often, benefits are sold to combat price, but they mean very little because they aren't sold constructively. Benefits should be illustrated so that they provide value to the product.

---

### THE CHILDREN'S BOOKS SELLING EXAMPLE
*Failing to overcome the product legitimacy barrier*

TSR: "I have a great item I know you are going to enjoy."

CUSTOMER: "That's all well and good, but how do I know I'll get everything you are telling me I am going to get?"

TSR: "I'd like to give you an idea what it's all about so you can see how wonderful it really is."

CUSTOMER: "Of course you would like to do that, but I've heard enough stories about telephone sales people, and I want to make sure that what you say I'm going to get is what I'm going to get."

---

The above scenario is extremely difficult to combat over the telephone, for many reasons. As we have touched upon before, telephone selling is a verbal medium of selling in a visual world. Customers today are so used to seeing products in person or on television or on the Internet, that creative imag-

**TELE-TIP**

The advantage the TSR has in his effort to regain control of the telephone presentation is that the TSR understands that direction of the presentation is extremely important. The customer has no idea about direction of telephone calls and maintaining control of conversations. Customers just talk, while maintaining direction is a component of telephone selling that the TSR makes an effort to succeed at.

ination has dwindled over time. This is where visual demonstration comes into play – if customers can't be creative, it is the job of the telephone sales rep to be creative for them. Another reason this is a tough scenario to overcome is because a customer's concerns about product legitimacy break down to the core of a customer's values. If a customer really doesn't feel comfortable making decisions over the telephone, then the customer is not going to be swayed to do so without the TSR first making an impact on changing that customer's <u>core values</u>. Perhaps the customer has been conditioned not to accept telephone solicitations, or perhaps the customer has been defeated in the past by telephone solicitors providing poor service. Maybe the customer is well read, and has been taught by the mass media to ignore telephone solicitations. In each of these situations, because the customer can't visually see the sales representative or the product being presented, the TSR has a long row to hoe. Below are rebuttals and questions that deal with product legitimacy.

"Ms. Jones, I understand your concern, and that is a concern of many of my customers. What do I need to do to reassure you that my product is legitimate?"

"Ms. Jones, I don't blame you one bit. What are some of the things I said that you are not comfortable with?"

"Because this product is designed to be sold over the phone, I'm not going to be able to show it to you unless you ask to see it. Does that make sense?"

"Can I offer you a call-back number so you can call the number and receive some assurances of the value of our product?"

"Ms. Jones, have you had poor experiences with telemarketing calls in the past?"

"I don't want you to miss out on this opportunity because of what may have happened in the past. What can I do to make my product worth your time?"

In each of the above examples, the goal is to get the customer to think a little more. Even if the initial reaction of the customer is to question whether the product is legitimate, the TSR must remember that an initial reaction is far from a final reaction! Assuming that a customer is interested in the presentation because he supplied the TSR with a specific objection, the TSR's goal is to keep the customer on the telephone for as long as he can. By regaining direction of the telephone call, the TSR literally begins the process of providing the customer with the necessary information to change his mind.

If the TSR can give the customer plenty of options, he can help the customer to think. Note that in the above rebuttals and questions, the TSR provides the customer with choices and options to open up new paths for the customer to take. One of the best ways to do this, and regain control of the call, is to ask questions that give the customer multiple choices, and spark multiple options. Based on the answers the TSR receives, he can begin the process of regaining direction of the call.

### HOW TO TRANSITION FROM THE PRIMARY OBJECTIVE TO THE SECONDARY OBJECTIVE

We spent a few moments earlier in this chapter discussing primary objectives and secondary objectives. My goal was to stress how important it was to have a primary objective on each call, because without primary objectives there would be very little focus. In addition, I emphasized that there may be and should be many secondary objectives to telephone calls, if for no other reason than the fact that in many telephone sales presentations it is the primary objective that gets eliminated early, and the secondary objectives that determine whether or not the call is successful.

Transitioning from a primary objective to a secondary objective is a challenge that involves three key criteria. The TSR must understand his product thoroughly, be extremely fast on his feet, and understand how his secondary objectives can benefit his customer as well as, if not better than, the primary objective.

**TELE-TIP**

If a customer really doesn't feel comfortable making decisions over the telephone, then the customer is not going to be swayed to do so without the TSR first making an impact on changing that customer's core values. Perhaps the customer has been conditioned not to accept telephone solicitations, or perhaps the customer has been defeated in the past by telephone solicitors providing poor service.

Here is an example. Imagine that the TSR is selling an insurance policy for all the electrical appliances in a customer's home. For $10.00 per month, the customer can have 24 hour repair service to the house on all major appliances. The primary objective is to close the sale, secure a credit card number, receive authorization, and finish the telephone presentation. Simple. Below are potential secondary objectives to that telephone sales call:

1. Gain commitment from the customer on a "bill me" basis.

2. Gain commitment from the customer that he will try the service out for 90 days on a "bill me" basis.

3. Gain commitment from the customer that he will try the service out for 90 days on an "as needed" basis.

4. Gain commitment from the customer that he will receive literature in the mail and consider the service. Call back at a later date.

If during the telephone presentation it is clear that the primary objective has gone awry, the TSR must swiftly convert to the first of his secondary objectives, and then make the transition from one secondary objective to another until he can get a solid commitment from the customer. Below are four steps to assist a TSR in transitioning from a primary objective to secondary objectives.

1. Prepare secondary objectives in an easy to follow format. Utilize index cards or a sheet of paper that clearly outlines every secondary objective.

2. Ask questions that lead into each of the secondary objectives. By asking questions, the TSR will cause the customer to think and respond, and a flow of conversation may develop.

3. Sell the benefits and features of the secondary objectives. As we will learn in a later chapter, benefits and features sell a program.

4. Set forth the simplicity of each secondary objective versus the initial complexity of the primary objective and other (rejected) secondary objectives. Customers may say "no" to a primary objective because it doesn't sound attractive. Not sounding attractive generally means it sounds complicated. As the TSR sells each secondary objective, he must compare its simplicity and attractiveness in relation to those objectives that were previously rejected.

# CHAPTER 6

## PROBES AND QUESTIONS

The man walked into a clothing store and saw an assortment of gorgeous men's suits. Some of the nicer suits cost more than he wanted to spend, while others that were noticeably different were on sale for a more suitable price. "I just don't want to spend that much money," the man said to himself as he perused the suit racks, going from those suits that were too expensive but stressed quality to those suits that fit his price range, but paled in comparison to the better suits. "I just can't make up my mind." At about that time, a sales associate entered the picture after studying the customer for the better part of five minutes. The sales associate had noted that the customer was scratching his head and checking price tags, always a sign that the customer was worried about price. At the same time, the sales associate noted that the customer was spending just as long in the expensive suit section as in the inexpensive suit section. This helped the sales associate realize that there was indecision on the part of the customer.

"Mr. Customer, how can I help you today?"

"I'm looking for a suit, but I'm not sure what kind I want."

"Let me ask you. Is it safe to say that you want to spend a certain amount of money?"

"Absolutely. No more than $500.00."

"Tell me, which color suit are you looking for?"

"Dark blue. I don't have a good dark blue suit."

"Is there a certain type suit you are looking for, such as double-breasted or three piece?"

"Double-breasted if I can afford it."

"Can I assume any particular maker, or just the best suit available for under $500.00?"

"Best suit available."

"Okay, let me re-cap to make sure I have everything correct. You want a new suit for under $500.00, double breasted, dark blue, best quality available for the price. Sound about right?"

"Yes."

What an easy customer to please, huh? What an easy sale? All the sales associate had to do was ask a few well placed questions and wham!!!!, the customer was ready to go. Actually, the purpose of the above example was not to demonstrate how to complete a sale. Instead, the purpose of the above example was to demonstrate how the TSR goes about gaining as much information as possible from the customer so the customer might best be helped to drop his indecisiveness regarding the purchase. In truth, the sales associate had little concern about completing the sale at the point of the questioning. His goal was to find out everything about what the customer <u>needed</u>.

The sales associate practiced a simple sales technique called "probing".

It is a universal technique practiced by every sales person in the world, regardless of whether the sales call takes place in person or over the telephone. By probing customers, the telephone sales representative learns everything he can about his customer and his customer's needs so he is better able to help the customer make the best decision. The best decision for the customer is, in most cases, the same decision the TSR is looking for the customer to make. Probing involves asking questions, discovering information, and then utilizing that information to the TSR's advantage as the TSR plans the sales presentation. In addition, probing is used by the TSR to assist the customer in focusing on what his needs and desires are. All successful telephone sales presentations succeed because TSRs ask their customers questions, and use the answers to those questions to sell their products.

## WHY PROBES ARE SO IMPORTANT

As we have noted in previous chapters, much of what goes into selling a customer over the telephone involves communicating the appropriate ingredients of the program to the customer. How does one find out which ingredients appeal to each customer? By asking.

The TSR who wants to find out as much information as he can about his customer is the TSR who is going to complete many sales over the course of his career. The truly great sales makers are those who know everything there is to know about their customers. Is my customer looking for this or that?

**By probing customers, the telephone sales representative learns everything he can about his customer and his customer's needs so he is better able to help the customer make the best decision.**

Does my customer need one or two? Is my customer looking to spend this amount or that amount? What product does my customer need? In each of these areas, the TSR can take a guess and try to establish what appeals to the customer. However, guessing is not accurate, and guessing often frustrates the customer.

Guessing what the customer needs is a sure-fire way to lose the sale. But asking the customer what he needs is a sure-fire way to complete the sale.

Let's analogize probing to other situations. In a relationship, the dating process is a form of communication that encourages questions and probes. If the questions and probes are answered successfully by both parties, the relationship continues. A first date is a prime example of a situation where probes dominate discussions. On most first dates, very little conversation takes place. Instead, most of the conversation is in the form of probes between both parties. Do you like movies? What kind? What types of food do you enjoy eating? Do you have brothers and sisters? How old are they? First dating defines basic probing.

For another example, in a first telephone call from a TSR to a customer, designed not necessarily to complete a sale but instead to establish a relationship, the art of probing is a necessity before generating a presentation. By probing the customer on his needs and wants, by asking the customer which benefits and features are likely to work for him, and by generating enough information to sell the themes, images and concepts of a product, the TSR is learning what it will take in future calls to complete the sale. What information needs to be provided? What areas of the program need to be emphasized? What aspects of the program need to be de-emphasized? How best can the TSR communicate the program to this customer?

Asking questions is not an easy discipline, because the ability to ask the customer questions is an art form that takes practice to perfect. A TSR shouldn't begin a telephone call by shooting questions from the hip as if they were bullets from a shotgun. If he were to do that, the customer would become afraid, uninterested, suspicious, and would lose any confidence he might have had about the sales process. After that, the TSR would not be able to make any headway and the potential for a sale would dissipate. Asking questions and probing the customer are difficult for another reason also.

Questions open up the opportunity for the customer to respond in a negative way. In my experience, TSRs are simply petrified that they might receive an answer from a customer that will completely devastate any possible sale. Certainly, this is going to happen, but that is no reason to eliminate probing from the sales presentation. Failing to ask a question that might elicit a negative response is like hiding one's head in the sand. If a customer has negative feelings and beliefs that will impede the chances of making a sale, it is best to learn this up front. At best, the TSR will be able to save the sale by confronting the belief. At worst, the TSR will have saved a lot of time for himself and the customer.

## FOUR TECHNIQUES WHEN ASKING QUESTIONS

Two of the important characteristics that make TSRs good probing artists involve listening and hearing. As we discussed earlier, listening and hearing are two traits that follow us everywhere in the telephone sales presentation.

When I discussed listening and hearing, I mentioned that listening and hearing are two principles of communication that make good TSRs exceptional. Here is how this ties into probing. As the TSR probes the customer, the customer is going to be supplying answers. It is important that the TSR listen to those answers so the customer feels that the TSR understands what he is saying. It is also important that the TSR hear those answers so he can figure out exactly what the customer means and what the customer needs and better approach the sales portion

**TELE-TIP**

A TSR can't just walk into a telephone call and start shooting questions from the hip as if they were bullets from a shotgun. If that happened, the customer would become afraid, uninterested, suspicious and lose any confidence he might have had about the sales process. The TSR would not be able to make any headway.

of the call. When the TSR listens correctly, he will make the customer feel as if he has an audience, and the customer will continue to talk. When the TSR hears correctly, he will understand what the customer needs and wants, and the sales presentation will move forward crisply. Probing moves the presentation forward, and listening and hearing properly complements the art of probing.

Another characteristic that makes TSRs good probing artists involves the *delicacy* of actually asking the questions. Sure, it is a given that the TSR needs to ask questions. However, the TSR must ask the right questions in the right way. This skill involves four techniques: Preparation, Rhythm, Inflection and Consistency.

● **Preparation**

Preparing questions is the prerequisite for asking powerful questions. Good questions don't just come flying out of a TSR's mouth without the preparation one might expect. TSRs should think intently about what needs to be asked prior to the telephone sales presentation. For example, I have found it best to make a list of twenty or twenty five probes, and rehearse them so that the TSR has five or eight general probes which he feels extremely comfortable utilizing. In addition, as certain topics of conversation arise in the telephone sales presentation, the TSR can review his twenty or twenty five probes and find the appropriate probe for the appropriate situation.

● **Rhythm**

Singers and dancers need rhythm, and so do telephone sales representatives. Establishing rhythm involves using strong listening skills. For instance, repeating back to the customer, in a question format, exactly what the customer said is an excellent way to ask a question and gain information while carrying on a very rhythmic conversation.

CUSTOMER:  "I really believe there aren't enough quality insurance salespeople in my office."

TSR:  "There aren't a lot of quality insurance sales people in your office?"

CUSTOMER:  "I can't believe I haven't been able to find a quality automobile."

TSR:  "You haven't been able to find a quality automobile? Why?"

If the customer expresses an answer or makes a statement and the TSR follows with a question that has nothing to do with the customer's subject matter, the call will lose any sense of rhythm, and the customer will feel as if he has not been heard. By instead utilizing the above way of responding to the customer, the TSR maintains the rhythm of the conversation and increases the rapport between himself and the customer.

● **Inflection**

Every question asked can be interpreted in a multitude of different ways, based upon the inflection of the question. Inflection becomes important when the TSR considers that the way a customer interprets questions sets the base for how those questions will be answered. Superb TSRs are capable of asking questions that sound, through their use of inflection, to be non-threatening, interesting and inviting of a response. "How do you like gun control?" is a simple question, but based on the way the TSR utilizes inflection, that question can be interpreted by the customer to sound inquisitive, sensitive, threatening, non-committal, persuasive, or all or none of the above.

"**How** do you like the peanuts?"

"How **do** you like the peanuts?"

**103**

"How do **you** like peanuts?"

"How do you **like** peanuts?"

"How do you like **peanuts**?"

After listing twenty to twenty five probes, the TSR must practice the manner in which he wants to ask each question, and decide how he will inflect each question. The TSR needs to recognize that the way in which the customer responds to a question may not be entirely based on how the customer feels or what he believes when he responds. It may be predicated more upon how the TSR inflects the questions, hence motivating the customer to respond. The TSR must condition himself to inflect questions appropriately, in order to elicit the desired response.

● **Consistency**

Managers who spend their days monitoring telephone sales reps may go through fits of mania when it comes to many TSRs' lack of consistency while probing. For example, a TSR may be asking a customer one or two dynamite questions, and the customer may be responding extremely well. All of a sudden, the TSR might swerve the rhythm of the conversation, and begin to probe whole different subjects, even when the present subject had yet to be completely exhausted! In a case like that the sales manager will always ask "What happened to the consistency of that call?" So will the customer. Once questioning begins on one subject, there should be little bouncing around to different subjects until questioning on the first subject is exhausted and the customer is aware that the subject matter of the questions is changing. A lack of consistency on the TSR's part will sink the telephone call. A basic tenet that I believe to be true is "the customer will be madly inconsistent throughout a telephone call." Because of this, it is all the more important that the TSR be tenaciously consistent with his probes. Following are six easy steps to ensure consistency when asking questions:

Ask each question in the same <u>even</u> manner

Ask each question in the same <u>even</u> style and format

Ask questions regarding one particular subject at a time

Ask questions until that one particular subject has been exhausted

Ask questions until the TSR has discovered all of the information he needs

Ensure that the customer is aware when particular subject matter and topics change.

The premise I base my telephone sales training on is that customers want predictability and consistency in order to feel comfortable. Thus, the TSR must give customers predictability in the type and style of questions asked. By mastering the above techniques, the TSR will be able to ask questions in a

**TELE-TIP**

Every question that can be asked falls into one of two categories. One category elicits from the customer general responses in an open setting (Open Probes), while the other category directs the customer toward particular answers to help inform the TSR of the customer's issues (Closed Probes).

way which will result in both parties being more comfortable, more relaxed, and better informed.

## TWO TYPES OF PROBES

The next step in successfully asking questions is to figure out exactly what kinds of questions are appropriate to ask, and the correct times to ask them. Every question that can be asked falls into one of two categories. One category elicits from the customer general responses in an open setting (Open Probes), while the other category directs the customer toward particular answers to help inform the TSR of the customer's issues (Closed Probes). By utilizing the correct type of question for each particular situation, the TSR will have a better chance of obtaining solid and quality information from the customer, to help the telephone sales presentation along.

## OPEN PROBES

Open probes are those probes designed to elicit as much information as possible from the customer. The objective of an open probe is to encourage the customer to communicate as freely as possible in an open setting. Open probes are used by the TSR to find out general information to assist in the sales presentation .

## BUZZ WORDS THAT BEGIN OPEN PROBES

Who

What

Where

When

Why

How

Did

Do

Tell me

## CHILDREN'S BOOKS SELLING EXAMPLE

*Below are examples of open probes for the sale of children's books.*

"Who else have you contacted regarding children's books?"

"Who else do you know of who reads children's books?"

"Where do you usually purchase your child's books?"

"Where do you think your child's reading level is at?"

"When are you considering purchasing children's books?"

"When can your wife make a decision?"

"Why did you subscribe with them?"

"Why have you not begun the process of ordering before?"

"What are you looking for in a children's book?"

"What do you plan to do to encourage your child to read?"

"How many hours does your child read each night?"

"How do you plan on purchasing books in the future?"

"Did you ever order children's books through the mail before?"

"Did your child find a certain type of book more interesting?"

"Do you think your child has an interest in action adventures?"

"Do you want to have your child read text-only books, or books with pictures as well?"

"Tell me, what are some of the things you need in a children's book club?"

"Tell me, how much are you willing to spend on a children's book series?"

## EXCELLENT OPEN PROBE QUESTION

**"How did you decide to buy your last children's book?"**

I have found this open probe question to be simple and results oriented. In telephone selling, TSRs often make their questions too complicated. This basic question obtains from the customer much of the information the TSR is going to need in order to eventually close the sale.

"I went to the local book store and I looked for real quality stories. I wanted to find books that looked like they were durable enough to last many years, because I plan to have more children in the future. Price wasn't an option."

With this information, the TSR has wonderful information as to what motivates the customer to buy. It can be assumed that if the customer was looking for certain factors when buying children's books in the past (quality stories, durable books, no price factor), those factors will exist when buying children's books today. The TSR can now begin selling his product based on the specifications the customer outlined in the answer.

## CLOSED PROBES

Closed probes are questions designed to elicit answers that are more direct and to the point. The TSR usually asks closed probes in a choice format, in an attempt to narrow down a customer's options. He also will use closed probes when he wants to convince the customer that there are only one or two options available, and when the TSR has a good idea how the customer will respond. These are questions that often lead to "yes" or "no" answers.

### BUZZ WORDS THAT BEGIN CLOSED PROBES

You

What

Is

How

Did

Do

Does

Will

Can

Are

Which

Have

Tell me

Has

## CHILDREN'S BOOKS SELLING EXAMPLE

*Below are examples of closed probes for the sale of children's books.*

"What do you like most about a book-it's story, content, or illustrations?"

"What do your children enjoy more, comics or action-adventure?"

"Is it safe to say your child enjoys reading more than writing?"

"Is television your children's favorite pastime, or is it reading or writing?"

"How many books do you purchase each month: two or three?"

"How will you purchase books over the telephone: through credit card or check order?"

"Did you ever purchase children's books from mail order before?"

"Has your daughter considered subscribing to a book club within the past three months?"

"Do you subscribe to more than four journals? Five? Six?"

"Do your children find more time to read on weekends or in the evening?"

"Does it make more sense to mail you the books now or after you have read the literature?"

"Does you husband have a say in the decision, or can you make that determination?"

"Will you be selling all of your other books, or keeping them?"

"Will your son be reading most of the children's books, or your daughter?"

"Can you purchase all of the books today, or would you just like to purchase one?"

"Can you decide on the size of the book you want by next Thursday?"

"Are you more likely to want your children to read fiction or non-fiction?"

"Are video games more important to your daughter?"

"Which is best for you, a savings in price or an additional book?"

"Have you considered purchasing books through the mail?"

"Have you been solicited by other telephone sales representatives before?"

"Tell me, what are the three things you are looking for in a children's book club?"

"Tell me, if you had to choose, would you want pictures or illustrations?"

"Has it ever occurred to you that you can purchase books through the mail?"

"Have your past subscriptions to book clubs been successes or failures?"

## EXCELLENT CLOSED PROBE QUESTION

"When buying children's books before, what was more of a factor: the price of the books, or determining which authors actually wrote the books?"

I have found this type of closed probe question to be simple and results oriented, because it frames the question around what the TSR needs to know. The customer, based on the way the TSR asked the question, is obligated to answer that either "price" or "authors" was more of a factor in his buying decision.

"When I bought books before, I looked at price. I figured that I didn't know one author from another anyhow, so it wouldn't matter to me who wrote the books. I also felt that, because I am on a budget, I was looking to bring home as many books as possible."

With this information, the TSR has wonderful insight as to what motivates the customer to buy. The TSR can now begin selling his product based upon the specifications the customer outlined in his answer.

Successful TSRs know when to use open probes and when to use closed probes. They are capable of switching their questions back and forth and then back again, depending on what is needed. They also have the talent to ask a few open probes in a row followed by a few closed probes, and vice versa, keeping a consistent rhythm. A TSR chooses open or closed probes based on <u>what the TSR needs</u> at the moment of the presentation to assist in his completion of the sale. If the TSR needs general information on a particular topic, he will ask an open probe geared to that topic ("Tell me, on the weekend, what sports do you play?"). If the TSR needs a specific answer on a particular topic, he will use a closed probe geared to that topic ("Tell me, would you rather play baseball on the weekend or football?"). In addition, a TSR chooses open or closed probes <u>based on how the customer responds</u> to the various probes. Some customers enjoy talking, which means open probes are a far better question format to utilize. Other customers believe in giving only one or two word answers, which means that closed probes fit that customer's style.

**TELE-TIP**

A TSR chooses open or closed probes based on what the TSR needs at the moment of the presentation to assist in his completion of the sale. If the TSR needs general information on a particular topic, he will ask an open probe, geared to that topic. If the TSR needs a specific answer on a particular topic, he will use a closed probe, geared to that topic.

Knowing which probes to use, how to use them and when to use them is an art form predicated on two factors. The first factor is instinct, which can't really be taught. The second factor can be taught, as it includes practice, knowledge, and skill development.

## WHEN AND HOW TO BEGIN THE PROBING PROCESS

The TSR was confident, on the cocky side, and he was also new at the job. I was monitoring the call as the phone was ringing, and I sensed the energy, excitement, and enthusiasm of the TSR. This was probably the first hour this TSR was on line.

TSR: "Hello, Ms. Smith?"

CUSTOMER: "Yes."

TSR "My name is Willie Jones from XYZ Company, and I have two questions for you. Where did you buy your last television set, and did you receive a warranty on it?"

CUSTOMER: "Good-bye."

**TELE-TIP**

In most telephone sales presentations, probing questions are designed to gather information so the TSR may understand what he needs to sell in order to complete the sale. In some instances, however, much of the needed information is obtained when qualifying the customer after the introductory period. Thus, probing takes on a more advanced nature.

Clearly, the TSR in the above example was a bit too enthusiastic, a bit too excited, and a bit unfamiliar with when and how to ask probes correctly. Most new TSRs are like this, however. They come in with tremendous energy and excitement, ready to "jump in the fire," and they forget that there is a science, and through this science a system to the madness.

I have found that probing really can't begin until after the TSR has identified himself and his program and established some sort of rapport with the customer. Earlier, we learned how truly important it is to establish some sort of bond with the customer prior to initiating the probing process.

After this bond has been established, the probing process is very simple. The TSR must begin the process in one of two ways: either by letting the customer know that questions are beginning, and why they are beginning; or by beginning the process of asking questions, with the understanding that the customer will catch on. Either style of probing works.

## COMMON PHRASES TO BEGIN THE PROBING PROCESS

"Mr. Smith, I'd like to ask you a few questions."

"Ms. Jones, in order to find out what is best for you, I need to ask you a few questions."

"Mr. Smith, let me ask you…"

"In order to better serve you, I have a few questions I need to ask."

"May I ask you a couple of questions, it will take less than a minute."

"I need to find out some information."

"To process your account information, I just need to ask you a few questions."

It is not important that the TSR spend a certain amount of time on the probing process, or that he establish a certain number of questions that will be asked. As for how they will be asked, there are two schools of thought on this, and I take the latter of the two positions. The first school of thought is that if the TSR says to the customer:

"I have only two questions to ask you"

"I have a few questions that will take only five minutes"

the customer will then hold the TSR to these time lines and become critical of the telephone call should it surpass these marks, which it always will. This school of thought also insists that credibility is on the line and the customer will lose confidence and trust should the TSR break these guarantees.

I say "hogwash" to this! I believe in the second school of thought, which dictates that customers don't hear 90% of what TSRs are saying anyway, so they certainly are not going to remember whether the TSR said "two questions" or "five minutes." The main concern is that the conversation develops proper rhythm and consistency and grasps the customer's attention. During such presentations the customer is too involved in the sales process to hold the TSR to the "five minute" mark. The key is that the TSR must have confidence in his ability to obtain and retain the customer's attention.

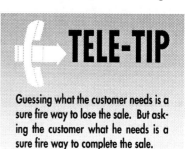

**TELE-TIP**

Guessing what the customer needs is a sure fire way to lose the sale. But asking the customer what he needs is a sure fire way to complete the sale.

## WHY WE PROBE THE CUSTOMER

It is valuable to understand the reasons why we are probing the customer.

To gain and maintain control of the conversation

To gather information

To sell the appropriate benefits and features and facts

To involve the customer in the "Feel" portion of the product

To understand the customer's needs, values and wants

---

### CHILDREN'S BOOKS SELLING EXAMPLE

"May I ask, which types of books do you purchase for your children?"
(Open Probe)

"What would you say is your yearly budget when it comes to buying books
for your children?" (Closed Probe)

"How have you purchased children's books in the past 12 months?"
(Open Probe)

"Would you say your children have liked or disliked the books you bought
for them in the past 12 months?" (Closed Probe)

---

In the above example, the TSR took two themes and stayed with them for four probing questions. Those themes were 1) Buying books for their children and 2) Buying books for their children within the last 12 months. By figuring out which questions he needed to ask, the TSR helped the customer to understand where the conversation was headed. Then the TSR used the answers to focus the customer on the appropriate theme.

---

### CHILDREN'S BOOKS SELLING EXAMPLE

*In this example, the TSR is going to ask probing questions designed to uncover which benefits and features might interest the customer as they relate to possibly buying children's books.*

"May I ask, is your child more interested in comic books or action books?"
(Closed Probe)

"What are some of your children's favorite storybook characters?"
(Open Probe)

"Does your child favor books of text or books of illustrations?"
(Closed Probe)

"What are some of the present titles your child owns?"
(Open Probe)

---

## COEN'S PARAMETERS TO PROBING

I teach eight fundamental parameters of probing.

### 1. Find the Right Time

It is so easy to ask a question at the wrong time. If the customer has something to say, don't interrupt his flow by asking a question. Let him speak. If the TSR is still developing rapport, asking fact-finding questions may appear to be aggressive and scare the customer away. Hear the customer intently and identify where the presentation is prior to beginning the probing process.

### 2. Begin with a Transition Phrase

We have all been involved in too many conversations with someone who kept shooting questions out in machine gun rapid fire, without setting the stage for those questions. It gets pretty irritating, because the questions come quickly, and there is little segue from one to another. When asking questions, it is important to lead into them as opposed to asking them outright. In this way, the customer understands more clearly what the TSR is asking and why he is asking it. Take this paragraph as an example. I could have started this paragraph with:

"When asking questions, it is important to lead into them as opposed to asking them outright."

Instead, I began it with this transition:

"We have all been involved in too many conversations with someone who kept shooting questions out in machine gun rapid fire, without setting the stage for those questions."

### 3. Don't Stumble

By asking a question, the TSR is giving the customer an opportunity to play "equal" with him in the sales conversation. Under this circumstance, the customer might give the TSR information that he may not be prepared to handle. So, since the TSR and his customer are now equals, it is mandatory that every question be presented in a secure and competent manner. Stumbling over the phone may cause the customer to see the TSR as confused, unknowledgeable, or insecure.

### 4. Use Inflection, Pace, Tone and Melody Appropriately

The words a TSR uses in a question are important. But the way he actually asks that question is even more important. Inflection, pace, establishing proper tone and utilizing melody all make the difference when probing customers.

**TELE-TIP**

Asking questions is not an easy discipline, because the ability to ask the customer questions is an art form that takes practice to perfect.

## 5. Ask Direct Questions

Customers don't want to be patronized and they don't want to be played with. Thus, when asking a question, just ask it. Don't beat around the bush, because that often sounds threatening to a customer.

## 6. Converse Between Questions

This is where establishing trust becomes so important. I mentioned earlier that shooting one question after another does no good without some sort of human interaction. Break up questions with comments and points of interest, even if those comments and points of interest don't appear to help validate the TSR's presentation. Conversing with the customer on a friendly level often creates a bond that will validate the presentation in the long run.

## 7. Be Patient

Probing questions work best when the TSR is in no apparent hurry to ask questions or to receive answers and move on. Customers have a strong sense that tells them when a TSR is hurried and anxious, wanting something quickly. When the TSR projects a lack of patience, the customer tends to follow suit, and that will destroy the telephone sales call.

## 8. Use the Customer's Responses

TSRs ask questions for a reason: the answers are supposed to assist the TSR in completing the sale. Customers don't *really* understand this basic fact – they think they are just responding to a question because the TSR asked it. Hence, if the customer answers a probe, the TSR needs to utilize the information received in any way possible to help him achieve the sale. Receiving responses without utilizing the wealth of information they provide is a terrible waste.

# CHAPTER 7

## SELLING BENEFITS AND FEATURES

I believe that selling benefits and features is the most interesting and exciting part of the telephone sales presentation, and I believe this because benefits and features add the color, the life, and the depth to the sales presentation. When we break a product down to its simplest core, a product is all about the benefits it can provide to customers, and the features of those benefits that customers can enjoy. In essence, benefits and features constitute the selling part of a sales presentation, because they involve a given: <u>people buy something and agree to do something when it is best for them to do so</u>. Selling benefits and features is the primary way to convince customers that accepting a product is the best thing for them to do.

In any field, selling benefits and features works. For example, a person accepts a job with a company because he is persuaded that the company will benefit him. Conversely, the company offers the job to him because it is persuaded that the person will benefit it. In this exchange, each side has been sold a benefit, and believes that the benefit is advantageous. In that same way, people get married because they are persuaded that the proposed mate is the one person they want to spend forever with, and business deals are brokered because two or more parties are persuaded that they will benefit from a transaction. Similarly, people buy fruit in a supermarket because they are persuaded that they will benefit from the fruit. In other words, nobody says "yes" without a reason, and that reason arises from the benefits and features that **persuade** the customer.

Many telephone sales reps find selling benefits and features a difficult proposition because it is in selling benefits and features that the telephone sales presentation becomes a challenging contest. Before benefits and features are sold, a product is bland. Customers have no reason to dislike or like the product. By opening up the world of benefits and features, the TSR is adding creativity, excitement and possibilities to the presentation. As in any situation where creativity, excitement and possibilities are created, there is always the chance that the response from customers might be negative.

In breaking down the art form of selling benefits and features, it is necessary to recognize the reasons why TSRs find selling benefits and features a difficult proposition:

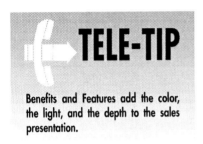

Benefits and Features add the color, the light, and the depth to the sales presentation.

*First*, customers may find fault with a program when its benefits and features are not persuasive (Of course, any customer who was happy with a program prior to the selling of benefits and features really didn't understand what the product was about anyway!). I have had a number of TSRs over the years ask me "Can't I just sell the product without mentioning the benefits? Every time I tell my customers why they should like the product, they don't like it." *Second*, customers see a door open up when benefits and features are illustrated, and this door allows them to ask questions, thus taking the direction away from the TSR and placing it with the customer. The TSR risks never regaining control of the conversation. *Third*, if benefits and features aren't persuadable, customers attempt to close the conversation swiftly right then and there, and the game becomes a tug of war to stay above water, rather than to make a sale. For example, if customers hear a few benefits of a product, with features to support those benefits, and then decide they don't sound attractive, the TSR may never have a chance to deliver the other benefits and features that might have been persuasive.

TSRs must recognize that no product offers every benefit and feature that the customer wants. For example, customers may love the idea that the TSR's long distance phone service has a better reputation than theirs does. However, when they don't receive a month of free service, volume discounts, or a lower gross rate per minute, customers might pull away from the sale. There is no panacea in telephone sales. The strength in benefits and features rests in the fact that they must appeal to customers by demonstrating the advantages of a product.

## HOW FEATURES SUPPORT BENEFITS

As we explore benefits and features, the goal for any TSR is to understand exactly how benefits and features co-exist in the sales process, and then learn how to sell benefits and features so they motivate the customer to buy. When TSRs attend different sales seminars, they learn that every sales trainer has a different philosophy on the cohesiveness and function of benefits and features in the telephone sales presentation. In the long run, this tends to confuse TSRs. With so many different philosophies and styles on the market, how can a TSR learn one that works? In reality, I believe strongly in the old adage that "more is better," and more philosophies and styles will only be beneficial for TSRs. Ideas are good, and ideas usually spawn off other ideas and create opportunities.

My philosophy contends that benefits drive the sales process and features provide support to the benefits. Hence, the objective for TSRs is to first sell the benefits of the product (big books, educational, inexpensive, and durable). Then the TSR should follow up those benefits with solid and credible features (easy to read, will improve a child's spelling skills, worth ten times its value, long lasting). In this way, the benefits are explained and then the features ensure that the benefits being sold are attractive. Benefits grab customers, and features provide stability and credibility which motivate the customer to appreciate the benefits. My philosophy visualizes benefits and features as a "team" which works together to grab, stimulate, motivate, and provide credibility for the customer.

Consequently, I believe the way to motivate the customer is to make benefits and features as credible and easy to understand as possible. Telephone sales is a credibility first medium. Without credibility, there will never be a sale. Each benefit must *mean* something to the customer for it to work, and quite often benefits by themselves don't mean much to the customer. Hence, features are used as a support mechanism of benefits to ensure that those benefits mean something. Features can be utilized as the credibility piece to make benefits shine. While benefits provide excitement and interest, features brace benefits with credibility and support.

## STEPS TO SELLING BENEFITS AND FEATURES

Uncover what the customer needs by asking questions

Always sell benefits first

Sell a benefit of the program that grabs the customer

Always sell features that apply to the benefit

Sell two or three <u>features of that benefit</u> that support the
benefit and motivate the customer

Ensure that the customer believes in the benefit and the features by
using the features as a credibility piece to support the benefit

## CHILDREN'S BOOKS SELLING EXAMPLE

*Uncover what the customer needs by asking questions*

"Ms. Jones, what are some of the things you are looking for in a children's book?"

"Can you provide me with a list of needs that you want fulfilled by your book store?"

"What would you like changed about children's books if you could make changes?"

*First, sell the proper benefit of the program to grab the customer*

"Ms. Jones, our children's books come with size 18 fonts."

"Our service provides a 24 hour book store delivery service."

"Our science fiction books come with fewer pictures than you are used to."

*Second, sell two or three <u>features of that benefit</u> to support the benefit and motivate the customer*

"With size 18 fonts, your child doesn't have to strain to read."

"Large fonts make learning to read quite easy."

"We provide the same amount of pages with the larger fonts."

"If your child doesn't have a certain book, we will deliver it 24 hours per day."

"Because no other book store has this delivery service, our quality stands out."

"Because we provide fewer pictures your child will use his imagination more."

"Less pictures means each page is full of more descriptive dialogue."

*Then, ensure that the customer believes in the benefit and the features by using features as the credibility piece to support the benefit*

"You explained your child was looking for larger font books. Can you see how our books fit your needs?"

"Our new 24 hour service has revolutionized this industry, providing the country with similar service in ten other states."

"What about more words and less pictures when it comes to science fiction books?"

To begin the process of selling benefits and features well, the TSR must learn seven critical steps:

## 1. Become organized before selling benefits

The TSR has a golden opportunity to sell his program well if he knows five or six wonderful benefits that make his program truly special. Every successful product has a minimum of five or six top-notch benefits. How TSRs view benefits differs greatly from one TSR to the next. (A TSR may think one benefit is more important to his product than another benefit, primarily because that TSR has had more success with selling that benefit than others ) To become organized before selling benefits, the TSR needs to take a piece of paper, and divide it into three columns. The first column represents benefits of the program; the second column represents the features which support those benefits; the third column represents facts of the program which support those benefits and features.

## 2. Prepare to answer a question with a succinct benefit

When customers ask questions, they want to hear answers. If the TSR provides answers that do not encompass a benefit, or provides benefits that are inconsequential to the question, the sale very well may be lost. Every question a customer asks needs to be answered with a succinct, focused benefit. In order to do this, the TSR should make a list of five or ten common questions that he expects will be asked by most customers and then prepare five or ten strong benefits (with a few features to support those benefits) to use consistently when answering those questions.

## 3. Become efficient in the explanation of benefits and features

Time is on the side of the customer. The customer doesn't want to be sold unless he feels that the time is right to be sold. The TSR must always understand what he is trying to express to the customer so the TSR doesn't waste his time. Long-winded essays and a lack of direction can stall the drive of a telephone sales presentation when the TSR isn't efficient and focused on his goal of selling.

## 4. Make benefits and features sound exciting and beneficial

The strength in benefits and features is that they motivate customers to *want* to buy a product, or at a very minimum to hear more about a product. In this respect, the TSR must sound enthusiastic in his delivery and paint a persuasive picture of how the benefits and features can help the customer. The TSR must make a point of emphasizing his benefits and features so that they stand out. The old adage is "sell, not tell," and this adage is appropriate to make benefits and features come to life.

## 5. Apply benefits and features to the customer's particular situation

Following our theme, benefits and features only become persuasive sales tools when the customer relates to them. Selling the benefit that local telephone calls can be free provides little benefits to a customer who doesn't own a telephone.

(It's a great benefit, but...) Finding out the customer's needs is a way to learn best which benefits and features apply to the customer. For example, it isn't enough just to say that power vitamins will make the customer feel better. That is a given. The TSR must literally take the way in which the customer is feeling now (i.e. lazy and unfocused) and relate that to what he will feel after taking the vitamins (i.e. dynamic and motivated).

### 6.  Differentiate between facts and benefits

TSRs have trouble in the very beginning of their careers learning the difference between a benefit and fact. A fact is something that clearly exists. "Mr. Jones, today you are presently paying $200.00 a month for your phone bill." A fact can also be persuasive, such as "Mr. Jones, I will only charge $160.00 for your phone bill." Facts are usually not glamorous, but they can be persuasive when used properly. In contrast to facts, benefits propel movement. It is the TSR's job to paint benefits as a work of art. Benefits are glitz and glamour that make a $40.00 savings in a telephone bill something worth acting upon. When is it best to use a fact? When the customer needs solid and easy to grasp credibility. When it is best to use a benefit? When the TSR needs to sell his product, motivate the customer and provide the customer with reasons to act.

### 7.  Differentiate between The TSR's favorite benefits and features and the Customer's favorites

Customers are not TSRs, and vice versa. TSRs tend to forget that what excites them doesn't necessarily excite the customer, and TSRs lose focus by concentrating on their needs and wants versus what the customer needs and wants. The TSR must determine which benefits and features the customer would like and then sell those to him. I have yet to hear of a TSR who can successfully sell benefits and features when the customer has zero interest in them.

### BENEFITS MUST INCORPORATE THE FOLLOWING SEVEN TRAITS TO INCREASE THE CHANCE OF COMPLETING THE SALE

Exciting

Surprising

Valuable

Educational

Persuasive

Expressive

Believable

## CHILDREN'S BOOKS SELLING EXAMPLE

*The above seven traits constitute the difference between quality benefits and mediocre benefits in a telephone sales presentation. Customers always fail to respond to benefits unless they include some aspect of the above seven traits.*

### Exciting

"Ms. Smith, these children's books give your child the opportunity that he has always wanted."

"Ms. Smith, the stories we wrote will take what usually takes months of reading and streamline that reading into days."

### Surprising

"Not many customers realize how special the photography is."

"In the past, books like these were only sold in stores. Today, they are offered through mail order as well."

### Valuable

"Reading is the lost art in society, but your child needs to have great reading skills if she will succeed."

"Normally, simple children's books don't provide the value that these do."

### Educational

"Within the last five years, the style of these books has undergone a much more scholastic approach."

"The stories your child will read today span three centuries of American history."

### Persuasive

"Our 30 day trial offer was implemented because we knew how much your child would enjoy these books."

"No other publisher on the West Coast has the same product line as we do."

### Expressive

"Pictures add to our books so that your child isn't bored by plain text."

"Over 50,000 children already have benefited from these books."

### Believable

"The publisher of these books has spent over 100 years working on books for children."

"We invite you to call our customer service hot line or contact some of our clients who themselves ordered these books through the mail."

## ONE LINERS WHICH LEAD INTO BENEFITS

One consistent sentence I communicate to TSRs is a truly simple sentence that encompasses a simple philosophy. "Go more slowly when you sell benefits." I have found that TSRs have the habit of communicating benefits to a customer as if they are apples spiraling down from a tree. Imagine that, all of a sudden and out of nowhere, the TSR begins to sell benefits to the unsuspecting customer without any set-up or explanation! (Imagine standing under an apple tree and having 500 apples drop upon you, with no warning!) When benefits are communicated en mass, customers become confused and benefits don't work.

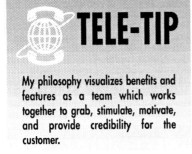

**TELE-TIP**

My philosophy visualizes benefits and features as a team which works together to grab, stimulate, motivate, and provide credibility for the customer.

To combat this dilemma, the TSR may introduce the fact that he is going to sell benefits to the customer prior to his doing so, and he may accomplish this by issuing a simple introductory one liner. *How* the TSR begins the process of selling his benefits can make more of an impact on the customer than the actual communication of those benefits. For example, customers subconsciously ask themselves the following questions while the TSR is selling benefits: was the TSR pushy when he started selling benefits? Did the TSR sound excited and enthused that he had benefits to sell? Did the TSR sound relaxed and confident that he knew exactly what he wanted to sell? Was the TSR able to explain that the benefits portion of the presentation was coming up?

TSRs can provide customers with positive answers by successfully utilizing the introductory one liner:

"Let me tell you…"

"If I can show you how…"

"I'm going to give you an example…"

"So many people feel the same way…"

"This is why we are different…"

"You are not going to believe this…"

"Would you believe…"

"I have something wonderful to tell you about this program…"

"Here is where we are different…"

"Listen to this…"

## THE CUSTOMER'S PERCEPTION OF BENEFITS AND FEATURES

Let's be perfectly clear on how selling benefits and features to one customer can differ completely from selling them to the next. There is an old saying in the sales world that the sales representative can't sell the same benefits and features to different customers, and the sales representative can't hold a grudge against a new customer because of the actions and reactions of the old customer. Selling benefits becomes increasingly difficult when customer aptitudes and attitudes change from one dial of the telephone to the next. Some customers may hear that the benefit of ordering a pizza early is that they will get it early, and that may ring as gold to them. On the other hand, other customers might hear that exact same benefit, and wonder why in the world they would want to order a pizza in the first place!

As a customer at home, I am sold benefits and features on the telephone all of the time, and quite often my perception is that they are misrepresenting their products and selling me trash. I hope, for the industry's sake, that I am wrong, but I know in some instances that I am correct in my assessment. The most important aspect of my thought process, however, is predicated upon the perception that the TSR is misleading me. Whether the TSR is or isn't misleading me doesn't matter. Whether I am right or wrong doesn't matter. Because I perceive that the benefits and features I am hearing are misleading, there is very little chance that I am going to allow the TSR to complete the sale.

Perceptions cloud reality all of the time, in every environment. When TSRs sell benefits and features, they are required to create a climate that gives customers the most positive perceptions possible. In this respect, below are four ways the TSR may manipulate how the customer *perceives* benefits and features so that the customer will accept his selling of benefits and features:

1.  **Don't sugar coat**

    Benefits and Features should be sold with sex appeal, but they should never be sold with more sex appeal than they are worth. Because establishing credibility is a large aspect of successful telephone selling, it becomes critical that the TSR doesn't get "carried away" with emphasizing the sex appeal of the benefits and features. Real good benefits and features can ride on their own.

2.  **Don't sound overly out of character**

    Because benefits and features are what sell a program, the customer tends to perceive their validity when they are <u>presented</u> with validity. A strong, authoritative approach to explaining a benefit or feature works tremendously better than a cautious, "I don't know if I'm correct" approach. In addition, once a sales presentation is initiated, it is important for the TSR to recognize that he has developed a character, and the customer has perceived this character throughout the entire presentation. Don't change that character!

## 3. Don't lose confidence

TSRs can easily lose confidence in themselves, their customers or their products at various times throughout a presentation. And for various reasons. This makes maintaining confidence all the more important. If a customer begins to sound disillusioned with a benefit or feature, the TSR can't assume all is lost – he must ask the customer exactly what the customer thought about the benefit or feature. What many TSRs will find is that their lack of confidence in some aspect of the presentation hindered the presentation far more than did the reality of the situation.

## 4. Probe the customer to make sure benefits and features are making an impact

Customer buy-in can't be underestimated. Customers will perceive that benefits and features are wonderful when TSRs make them buy in to the fact that they are wonderful. After presenting a few benefits and features, the TSR should ask the customer what he thought of them. If they were liked, the mission was accomplished.

## THE IMPORTANCE OF SILVER BULLETS

In the course of telephone sales presentations, it is logical that TSRs tend to utilize those benefits and features that they feel are particularly strong indicators of their program. I call these "silver bullets," because they are the dominant benefits and features that most often persuade a customer to say "yes" to the program. These are the premier benefits and features of a product. Below are my philosophies on how best to use these strong "silver bullets" in a telephone sales presentation.

- **Identify three or four "silver bullets"**

    Every program has benefits and features that end up in two classes. The first class (and the distinctive class) is the "silver bullets" class. In this class exist the best and brightest benefits and features that most often convince customers to buy the product. These benefits and features should be placed in a special corner, and the TSR should make an effort to categorize them separately from all of the rest.

- **Keep "silver bullets" hidden until needed**

    I am a big believer that the best benefits and features shouldn't be expressed to the customer until the TSR has ascertained that he needs to do so. Good TSRs have learned to sell well using secondary benefits and features. A devil's advocate would say that if the TSR really wants to make a sale he should use his best ammunition first (his silver bullets), and I would agree to that. But if the customer isn't warmed up to the product offer, then throwing the silver bullets out too early in the conversation will waste their usefulness. The TSR needs to judge *what* the customer needs, and then sell the appropriate benefits accordingly. However, for as long as possible, he should withhold the silver bullets.

# TELE-TIP

If a customer begins to sound disillusioned with a benefit or feature, the TSR can't assume all is lost—he must ask the customer exactly what the customer thought about the benefit or feature.

- **Adapt "silver bullets" per prospects**

Although the TSR has three or four outstanding general benefits that he can use as "silver bullets" at any time, the TSR also has "silver bullets" that correspond to each individual customer. For example, if the TSR is talking to a customer about different mutual funds available to the public, and the customer insists that he is looking for mutual funds within the science and technology fields, then it is clear that the "silver bullets" the TSR can utilize are those benefits and features that relate to the science and technology fields. In addition to the three or four general "silver bullets", specific "silver bullets" may be classified as any benefits and features that appeal in the best way to a particular customer.

## ORGANIZATION OF BENEFITS AND FEATURES

As we have explored, selling benefits and features is fun and exciting because they are the glamour and substance that sell a program. Look around at various telephone sales projects and see what sells the programs. In doing so, it is quite easy to identify the benefits and features of those programs!

Organization is an imperative when selling benefits and features. It has been my misfortune to see far too many disorganized TSRs absolutely destroy their chances for success because they didn't have the wherewithal to organize their benefits and features. Below are two tips to help TSRs organize their presentation of benefits and features to the customer:

1. **Utilize Index Cards**

   The TSR should list his silver bullet benefits and features and another five or ten strong benefits and features on different index cards. The cards should be used like flash cards around the TSR's desk. Example:

---

**CARD #1**

*BENEFIT*

Joining "The Club" saves $40.00 per month on auto and home repair

*Feature #1*

Can use that money to invest in stocks and bonds

*Feature #2*

Can receive travel vouchers good for free hotels

*Feature #3*

Can be confident of 24 hour, seven day a week repairs

---

2.  **Each Desk should have a Benefits and Features page**

    This is an important step for any telephone sales project. A benefits and features page is a page that lists every benefit and feature associated with a program. The "at-your-finger-tips" organization will allow the TSR to make a more confident presentation.

---

**BENEFITS AND FEATURES PAGE**

*BENEFIT*

By purchasing the shampoo today, you will be guaranteed to have fresher hair

*Feature #1*

You will look more confident

*Feature #2*

You will appear more professional

**BENEFIT**

Fresher hair means better health

*Feature #1*

Less chance of losing your hair

*Feature #2*

Less chance of becoming gray around the sides

---

# CHAPTER  8

## TRIAL CLOSING AS THE MEANS TO SUCCESS

When it comes to the telephone sales presentation, the TSR and the customer are in agreement on one primary point: neither the TSR nor the customer are prepared to close the sale until they know it is the right time to do so. From the TSR's perspective, he wants to attempt to close the sale only in one of two circumstances. One circumstance is when he feels relatively certain the customer will respond positively to that attempt. The other is when he feels that the sales call is not going the right way and wants to see how the customer will respond to a closing question. From the customer's perspective, he will agree to close a sale only when he feels it is right for him to do so. This usually comes about when the customer feels emotionally that he is comfortable with what he has heard, or when the customer has received enough logic (data) to make him feel correct in doing so (in the chapter that covered emotions versus data, remember that customers make decisions based on emotion, and use data to support that emotion).

The way both parties come to the same conclusion depends upon the TSR's ability to successfully trial close throughout a sales presentation. Trial closing throughout a telephone sales presentation involves asking the customer leading questions in a style that falls short of completely closing the sale, in order to make sure the telephone sales presentation is moving in the correct direction. In addition, trial closing can be used to persuade the customer to feel that the telephone sales call is moving in the correct direction. Trial closing ties into the basic concept that maintaining control of the telephone call, from start to finish, is critical for success. The TSR must be able to maintain direction of the telephone sales presentation at all times, especially as the call comes down the home stretch, and asking trial closing questions throughout the telephone sales presentation provides the TSR with a greater opportunity to maintain direction and sell the customer.

## DEFINITION OF TRIAL CLOSING

The definition of a trial close helps to enlighten the telephone sales representative with regard to what the trial close is best used for. In Webster's Dictionary, 1993, *trial* constitutes "examination by a test" while close constitutes "to come to an agreement; to shut; to finish." By asking trial closing questions, the TSR is attempting to "test" the customer on various subjects that are important to the success of the sales presentation. In addition, by trial closing, the TSR is conditioning the customer to "agree" to the TSR's theories, in order for the TSR to feel comfortable that actually closing the sale will result in a positive response. If the customer responds positively to trial close questions, then the TSR may assume that the customer is being swayed in the direction of the presentation, and this direction will lead to a sale. On the other hand, if the customer provides responses to trial close questions that the TSR wasn't expecting or didn't want to hear, then the TSR is made aware that he needs to maneuver the sales presentation back on to a different path in order to salvage the presentation.

Trial closing is a meaningful and considerably challenging element of telephone sales that every TSR must utilize in order to be successful. Unfortunately, my experience has shown me that most TSRs have difficulty when it comes to trial closing their customers, for a variety of reasons.

**TELE-TIP**

The way both parties come to the same conclusion depends upon the TSR's ability to successfully trial close throughout a sales presentation.

*First,* TSRs don't completely understand how trial closing can make the difference between a presentation ending in success or a presentation ending in failure. Certainly, they have the concept that gaining and maintaining direction of the telephone call is important. They also have the concept that the customer must "buy-in" to what the TSR is trying to sell. But they haven't proven to themselves that asking the customer trial closing questions, and conditioning the customer toward the close will make a difference in their success rate. *Second,* I believe that TSRs don't realize how critical conditioning the customer to say "yes" is, and they don't understand why conditioning the customer to say "yes" will make a difference in their success rate. In the chapter regarding conditioning, I made the point that we, as members of society, are conditioned all of the time and have been conditioned all of the time to react and act certain ways. Perhaps we have been conditioned not to understand our own conditioning, which is why TSRs have been conditioned *not* to trial close. Yet in the telephone sales presentation, getting the customer to say "Yes" or "I agree" or "Continue" makes all the difference in the world when the TSR begins the final closing process. *Third,* I believe TSRs fail to grasp the true importance of the trial close and the benefits the trial close can bring to a telephone sales presentation because they aren't trained repetitiously on how to trial close well. Most TSRs believe the trial

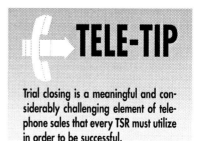

**TELE-TIP**

Trial closing is a meaningful and considerably challenging element of telephone sales that every TSR must utilize in order to be successful.

close is a huge dinosaur that is insurmountable to control and doesn't warrant the effort to try. Oftentimes, when I talk to a TSR about the importance of trial closing, he will say "Yeah, I know it will help me make more money, but I really don't think it works on this project." That is an excuse for "I really am afraid of trial closes and don't want to do them." In truth, trial closing throughout a telephone sales presentation is fun and it's easy, especially when the TSR has done an exceptional job of selling the other parts of his sales presentation (such as benefits and features, qualifying questions, probing questions, etc.). All the intimidation of trial closing dissipates when the TSR grasps how much value trial closing adds to a telephone sales presentation.

And trial closing works on *every project.*

As an example, I remember when I was once one of the most stubborn telephone sales representatives among a group of about twenty of us. For weeks, both during my initial training and then throughout my stay at this company, my manager poked and prodded me to learn how to trial close successfully. It wasn't that I couldn't trial close, because I knew how to do it from a fundamental perspective. My lack of trial closes had very little to do with the fact that I thought I could make more sales by not trial closing. I knew, deep down inside that I could increase my number of sales and my income by trial closing. Yet, I refused to do it. Certainly, I could see the frustration in my manager's face each time she sat down with me and reviewed my call performance. She couldn't figure out why I wouldn't trial close, when I had demonstrated in every training setting that I was excellent at it.

Finally, I took her aside and let her in on my secret. "The reason I don't trial close," I said sheepishly, "Is that I am scared that the customer is going to slam me when I do it." The cat was out of the bag, and I will never forget that experience. My fear of the unknown was stopping me from making more money and becoming more successful.

## FOUR REASONS TO TRIAL CLOSE THROUGHOUT THE TELEPHONE SALES PRESENTATION

There are four primary reasons why a TSR trial closes throughout the telephone sales presentation.

### 1. To Gain And Maintain Direction Of The Telephone Call

By trial closing the prospect, the TSR can move the prospect exactly where he wants that prospect to go. As we discussed earlier, gaining and maintaining direction of the telephone call is absolutely critical for achieving success. When the prospect maneuvers the call to where he wants that call to go, the TSR maintains some semblance of control. Persuasive trial closing questions keep the direction of the call intact.

> "You like the one pound, don't you? I'd like to stay with our one pound discussion instead of the two pound discussion."

> "You are more likely to purchase a hamburger today aren't you? Then, let's talk about hamburgers."

### 2. To Gain The Customer's Commitment

It is universally agreed upon by telephone sales trainers that telephone sales representatives often make the fundamental mistake of asking for the sale before they even know if the customer is interested in saying "yes" to the question. In other words, TSRs have the graceless habit of closing too early, without first setting up the close with valuable trial closing questions. By sheer logic, it is more important for the TSR to find out *prior* to the close that the customer is committed to what the TSR has been telling him than to find out after the TSR goes into the close.

This brings us to the importance of gaining the customer's commitment prior to the close. Gaining the customer's commitment by utilizing trial closing questions involves motivating the customer to say "yes" as often as possible to questions that directly relate to the presentation, the customer, and the product. Of the four reasons to trial close throughout a telephone sales presentation, trial closing to gain a customer's commitment is the most popular reason TSRs use the trial close. If, for example, the TSR asks the customer five questions about topics they explored, and the customer answers affirmatively to all five questions, then it is safe to say that the customer would be more likely to agree to a closing statement by the TSR, because the customer has been conditioned to do so. Not only can the TSR use the customer's "yes" responses as a way to remind the customer of his interest when the presentation

**TELE-TIP**

Selling benefits, features, and facts may be enhanced when the TSR asks the customer a trial closing question to confirm that there is agreement between the two parties.

reaches the close ("Mr. Smith, I know you are not interested in light bulbs right now, but you were twenty minutes ago"), but the TSR can also use those "yes" responses as a way to **condition** the customer to respond positively to what the TSR says in the future. When the TSR can condition the customer to accept what the TSR is saying, as well as gain the customer's commitment throughout the telephone call prior to the close, the TSR has moved an incredible step forward toward finishing the sale.

It is important at this point to remember a simple fact: <u>The customer has more confidence in what he says than in what the telephone sales representative says</u>. Thus, the TSR can try a trial close question: "I feel the purple raincoats are the nicest coats in the world, don't you?" But if the customer really doesn't **say** he agrees with that statement, then the statement becomes useless. "Yes, Mr. TSR, I'm glad you feel the purple raincoats are nice. Why don't you buy one, because I'm not going to."

In telephone sales, customers find it much easier to say "no" to a question than to say "yes". Our society has taught customers on the other end of a telephone sales presentation to "think" two thoughts right off the bat. **First,** that they are going to say "no" to any offer. **Second,** that they are going to continually reject offers over and over again until the sales person realizes he must move on. This isn't a theory on my part – it is a fact. Each time a telephone sales representative calls a customer at home or work, the customer's first inclination is to say "no". Fear encompasses a large part of our society, and the fear of the unknown transcends this. Customers immediately think three thoughts regarding the TSR in the initial stages of a phone call: that the TSR is out to make money at the expense of the customer, take money from the customer, and sell the customer a product that he doesn't need. There are very few customers who actually relish the prospect of receiving a telephone sales solicitation. Because of this, there are very few customers who go into a telephone sales presentation with the thought that they are going to say "yes". For example, I recently had a door-to-door salesperson visit my home and try to sell me a new type of carpet cleaner. Right when I saw who he was, I backed away from the door five inches, swung the door shut five inches, and decided before he said who he was that I wasn't going to accept his offer. I was thinking "no" and "rejection, rejection, rejection" right from the start. He didn't help his case, either, because I considered him rude, obnoxious, and unwilling to listen to anything I had to say. Unlike customers who can easily slam the telephone on the receiver and put an end to the conversation quickly, however, I couldn't slam the door in his face because I didn't want to be rude to him. In person, it is much harder to be rude to somebody and say "no" than it is over the telephone, because the intimate contact of a personal visit forms some kind of bond. Sure, I **did** eventually close the door on him, but it took awhile, because I didn't want to be impolite. Over the phone, however, if the TSR were rude, obnoxious and unwilling to listen to anything I had to say, I very easily, with no qualms, could have hung up the telephone. This explains why the TSR must get that commitment and conditioning from the customer. The TSR needs to remember that upon picking up his telephone, the customer is thinking "no." <u>By</u>

gaining "yes" commitments and allowing the customer to condition himself to saying "yes" over and over again, the TSR is maneuvering the customer away from his initial thought process and motivating the customer to more likely than not agree to the sale. For this very reason, gaining the customer's commitment early is critical when selling via the telephone.

---

### CHILDREN'S BOOKS SELLING EXAMPLE

*Gaining the customer's commitment*

"Are you happy with the books I told you about?"

"Are the stories I mentioned something your son would like to read this month?"

"Don't you think these children's books are a wonderful educational tool?"

"Can you see how the illustrations in these books provide special meaning to children?"

*Conditioning the Customer through Commitment*

"Your children would be happy with the books, stories, and illustrations, wouldn't they?"

"Isn't it true you told me your son likes science fiction?"

"When we spoke yesterday, you told me that price was not a factor, right?"

---

3. **To Confirm That The Customer Is In Agreement With Benefits And Features**

   Trial closing is a wonderful way to find out what the customer is looking for in the way of benefits and features. More importantly, it is a way to confirm that the benefits and features which the TSR sold to the customer indeed are the benefits and features the customer is looking for. Obviously, if they aren't, it is best for the TSR to start over. For example, let's say a telephone sales rep sells phone service. If the TSR explains to the customer two benefits about that phone service and then asks a trial closing question such as "Do you believe as I do that these two benefits would save you money?" the TSR is motivating the customer to confirm to him that the benefits were successful. How was the TSR to know whether the customer enjoyed the benefits without asking a trial closing question after selling the benefits? If the customer agrees that those two benefits can save him money, the TSR then can bring those two benefits up later in his conversation as reasons why the customer should say "yes". If he disagrees with the TSR, the TSR now understands not to bring up those benefits again, because in this customer's eyes, those benefits are worthless.

   Selling benefits and features may be enhanced when the TSR asks the customer a trial closing question to confirm that there is agreement between the two parties. This becomes more and more obvious as telephone sales representatives begin to realize how ambiguous benefits and features are to a customer. A customer may like what the TSR doesn't like, and vice versa. Even probing the customer prior to selling a certain benefit, feature or fact only works so far, because what the customer may have agreed to when asked a probing question can turn out to be quite different when the TSR asks a trial closing question. For example, suppose a TSR in the probing part of his presentation asks the customer whether he would be happy with a flat minute rate for his phone service. The customer responds "yes". Then, the TSR goes forth and sells the benefits of his program, one benefit of which is that his flat rate is only 10 cents per minute. If the TSR lets that segment end there and moves on, the TSR won't be sure whether the customer really was happy with the 10 cents per minute rate. The TSR may think the customer is happy, but he doesn't know for certain. However, if the TSR then asks "A rate of 10 cents per minute is acceptable to you, isn't it?" the TSR will know for certain whether or not there is agreement on that benefit.

## THE CHILDREN'S BOOKS SELLING EXAMPLE

*Confirming the customer is in agreement on benefits, features and facts*

"Ms. Smith, don't you believe those children's books are worth $30.00?"

"Mr. Smith, hardback covers are critical for children, aren't they?"

"I like the books that provide children with historic data, don't you?"

"Isn't it fun to think that over 50,000 children have already experienced these books?"

When asking trial close questions after the TSR sells benefits and features, it is important for the TSR to recognize different buying signs from the customer as the customer attempts to provide answers. Buying signals from the customer can make a success of a telephone call, but more often than not they break a telephone call. Why? Because when the TSR doesn't recognize a clear buying signal from the customer, the TSR misses the moment in time when the customer was motivated to say "yes", and that moment may not come around again. Also, if the TSR doesn't look out for buying signals, he won't know if he received any, and not receiving a buying signal is a sure sign that the telephone sales call is going awry. Buying signals are those signals from the customer that TSRs really must work at hearing. For example, within most presentations where a sale can be made, telephone sales trainers will say that they heard a multitude of buying signals. I oftentimes monitor telephone sales representatives and hear ten or eleven buying signals on the telephone when they hear none. Were they looking for them? No. Were they aware of what to look for? No. Could they have used some of the customer's buying signals and jumped on them? Absolutely. Did the TSRs know that they had missed buying signals? No. Customer buying signals may span from silence on the customer's part, to rapid talking, to a direct statement by the customer expressing an interest in an aspect of the presentation that he is hearing. In addition, buying signals can be presented in the form of objections

**TELE-TIP**

While probing is the information element of the telephone sales presentation, trial closing is the conditioning element of the telephone sales presentation.

from the customer with an opening so the TSR can prove his case. Or, buying signals can be comments from the customer about an aspect of the TSR's product. When the TSR utilizes trial closing questions, the customer tends to give off buying signals in droves when he is interested. Obviously, when he is not interested, he gives off very few signals at all. A capable telephone sales representative will utilize his hearing skills to recognize buying signals, and then move on from there. The reason buying signals are so prevalent upon the TSR asking a trial close question is because the customer is more apt to give a straight and honest response to a trial close question than to any other question. If the response is positive, the TSR will hear a buying signal and jump on it. If the response is negative, the TSR will not hear a buying signal and will try to correct it. With a trial close question, the TSR is leading the customer to make a statement of commitment about the benefits, features or facts that the TSR just sold. The answer the customer gives the TSR has buying signals written all over it. It is the responsibility of the TSR to be very meticulous in hearing those buying signals and recognizing their value.

**4. To Motivate The Customer To Accept The Final Close**

There are two types of final closes: those that work, and those that don't. Almost all of the final closes that work come after the TSR has trial closed the customer throughout his presentation. Certainly, conditioning plays a large role in this, but trial closing in order to motivate the customer to accept the final close stems from more than just conditioning. If, throughout a presentation, the customer is motivated by the trial closes he is responding to, then it is highly likely that the customer is going to be motivated by the final close, as well. This part of selling, known as the "set-up", is absolutely mandatory for success. Watch other sales people practice this set-up, from the car salesman down the street to the clothing salesperson, and so forth. It is far too difficult to motivate the customer to say "yes" on his own, without the set-up.

### WHEN TO USE THE TRIAL CLOSE

The trial close is a skill that the TSR can't use just any time he wants to. Trial close questions are best used throughout the latter portions of the telephone sales presentation, when the TSR is most concerned about solidifying his sales presentation and moving the sales presentation toward the close. Trial closing takes place throughout the latter one-third of a telephone sales presentation, after the TSR has established some form of relationship with the customer, learned some information about the customer, and delivered some benefits and features about the product.

Below are the stages of a telephone sales presentation that should be completed *prior* to utilizing a trial closing question:

Introduction

Qualification

Probing

Selling of Benefits and Features

The TSR must be assured that he has maneuvered past the above four stages before he begins the trial closing process. Assuming the TSR has already qualified the customer, probed the customer for information and sold various benefits and features of his program, a bond will have been established. If the bond is tenuous, a strengthening of the relationship is in order, or a trial close question may turn the customer off completely from the presentation. However, if the bond is solid, the time is right for a trial close question.

What would happen if there were no bond between the customer and the TSR, and the TSR asked a trial close question anyway? What would happen if the TSR were to trial close earlier within the telephone sales presentation? The customer probably wouldn't have enough of what he needs to give the TSR the responses the TSR is looking for. For example, it is impossible

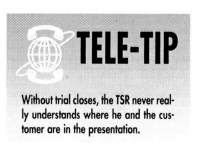

**TELE-TIP**

Without trial closes, the TSR never really understands where he and the customer are in the presentation.

for a waiter in a restaurant to trial close his customers on their favorite menu items before his customers have had a chance to review the menu. Hence, when it comes to trial closing questions, early is not always better. It is imperative that the TSR move through the qualifying, probing, and most of the benefits and features segments of his presentation before he begins to trial close.

## HOW TRIAL CLOSING DIFFERS FROM PROBING

Initially, many TSRs get confused between trial closing and probing, and that makes sense. Both trial closing and probing involve asking the customer questions to find out information that will assist the TSR in the future. That is where probing and trial closing are most alike. The greatest difference between the two is that probing always, in every telephone sales presentation, comes before trial closing. First, the TSR must probe the customer for information. Then, the TSR must tie in that information, sell benefits and features, and follow that selling process with trial closes to ensure that the customer and the TSR are on the same path, moving toward the close. While probing is the part of a telephone sales presentation where the TSR finds out information from the customer so he can use that information in the future to sell the customer, trial closing takes this a step further by becoming more of a semi-closing process. While probing is the information element of the telephone sales presentation, trial closing is the conditioning element of the telephone sales presentation. The importance of trial closing is magnified because, without trial closes, the TSR never really understands where he and the customer are in the presentation. Does the customer like the benefits and features that he heard? Is the customer still interested in the product? Will the customer consider any of the benefits and features mentioned? Is the customer more inclined to order factory items in red or in black? Do long term items appeal to the customer? These are all questions for which trial closes can secure the answers.

## HOW TO TRIAL CLOSE

The simplest use of a trial close question in a telephone sales presentation is to state a benefit, feature or fact, and come back with one of the following questions:

"Wouldn't you agree?"

"Isn't it true?"

"Don't you think so?"

"Doesn't that make sense?"

"Can you see the benefit of?"

These five trial closing questions get customers involved in the conversation, and lead customers on the road toward agreeing with what the TSR is saying. In addition, these trial closing lines allow the TSR to see where he stands. It is very important that after stating a benefit or feature, the TSR motivates the customer to express his thoughts about the benefit or feature by offering one of these five trial closing questions.

These five questions can be used in a variety of different ways. They can be used at the beginning of a trial close, the middle of a trial close, or at the end of a trial close, depending on how the TSR wants to ask the question.

## CHILDREN'S BOOKS SELLING EXAMPLE

*State a Benefit or Feature – Trial Close*

"The children's books come in red, yellow or green. <u>Don't you agree</u> those are three fantastic colors to choose from?"

"Mr. Jones, <u>can you see</u> how your child will have countless years of entertainment because of these books?"

"<u>Wouldn't you agree</u> that the imaginary characters will provide a level of science fiction your child can't get from television today?"

"<u>Doesn't that</u> thirty day trial offer make sense?"

"Your child is an avid reader of large text books, <u>isn't it true</u>?"

## EXAMPLES OF TRIAL CLOSING QUESTIONS THAT CAN BE USED OVER THE TELEPHONE

"Doesn't it make sense to…"
"Based on the benefits we chatted about, doesn't it makes sense to…"

"Don't you agree…"
"Don't you agree that the features of this program…"

"Isn't it time that…"
"Isn't it time we picked a place to meet…"

"Wouldn't it be worthwhile…"
"Wouldn't it be worthwhile to explore more of this element of my product…"

"Don't you feel that…"
"Predicated on what you heard, don't you feel that…"

"Can you see the advantage of…"
"Mr. Jones, can you see the advantage of…"

"Are you excited by the fact that…"
I was wondering, are you excited by the fact that…"

"Isn't it great to know…"

"Have you considered the fact that…"

"Wouldn't it be great if…"

"Doesn't it make you feel good that…"

"Won't it be gratifying when…"

"Can you see the benefit of…"

"Did you like the fact…"

"In your opinion…"

"If you were to…"

"Do you prefer…"

"If I (benefit, feature or fact)…will you?"

This can be both an open or closed-ended trial close question, depending on how the customer responds. The bargaining with the customer allows you to find out what works, but the customer may respond with more than you bargained for. In any event, it is an information-gathering device as well.

### TRIAL CLOSING ONE LINERS

"I'd like to tell you about our subscription plan. But first, did you like the fact that our program offers so many benefits?"

"Wouldn't it be great if each of your children could utilize the science fiction stories?"

"The return postage is something many subscribers like. Can you see the advantage of our return postage policy?"

## THE TRIAL CLOSE SHOE LACE

Trial closing becomes fun in many additional ways, too. Trial closes don't only encompass one or two sentences in order to be effective. They can also be just two or three words:

"Aren't they?"

"Can't you?"

"Shouldn't we?"

"Isn't it?"

"Okay?"

"Won't you?"

"Wouldn't you think?"

"Didn't it?"

**CHILDREN'S BOOKS SELLING EXAMPLE**

*Trial Closing Shoe Lace*

"The hard covers make them attractive, <u>wouldn't you think</u>?"

"<u>Can't you see</u> why children have flocked to our novels?"

"<u>Isn't it</u> fascinating?"

"Your children are reading above average, <u>aren't they</u>?"

# CHAPTER

# THE TELEPHONE CLOSE –
# THIS IS WHAT IT'S ALL ABOUT

Imagine for a moment that customers of all shapes and sizes pass through a permanently open door. Without any reason to stop or ponder, these customers merely walk to the door, smile, and walk through the door. The door is merely a channel between one area and the next.

In the telephone sales presentation, one of the goals of the TSR is to open these very doors for his customers, so they can see new areas and learn how those areas are beneficial to them. The areas that customers learn about provide the meat of a telephone sales presentation. However, an open door that never closes is a door that will sink the telephone sales presentation, over and over and over again. No matter how motivational or successful it may be for a TSR to open doors, the only way to motivate customers to do what the TSR wants them to do is for the TSR to *close those doors.* Leaving the doors open at the beginning of a telephone presentation may be okay, but leaving them open (so the customer can leave any time) at the end of the telephone presentation constitutes bad telephone selling.

Closing the customer and completing the sale is the reason a telephone sales presentation is delivered, and this fact is brought home to TSRs only after they realize that closing the customer is the only way to finish the sale. No matter what type of presentation is delivered, the fact remains that each telephone sales call attempts some kind of close, to complete the objective of the conversation. The close may be an order for money, an invitation to join a club, an agreement to schedule an appointment, a relationship building exercise preceding a later call. In each situation, the telephone presentation has some kind of close to complete the objective of the conversation.

Opening doors throughout the sales presentation and closing doors at the end of the presentation is the paradox of selling over the telephone. On the one hand, the TSR must work extremely diligently to open doors so his customer may gather all of the information he needs in a non-threatening environment. At the drop of a hat, however, the TSR must begin to work even more diligently to close doors so his customer will feel motivated to make the decisions the TSR wishes him to make. This paradox can be challenging to TSRs, and it is confusing for customers. In any event, top-notch TSRs find this paradox fascinating, and they find the science behind succeeding at telephone sales even more fascinating.

With the above in mind, the whole concept of closing over the telephone can be focused upon three techniques:

> TSRs must open doors at the beginning of the presentation

> TSRs must encourage customers to go through doors in the middle of the presentation

> TSRs must close doors at the end of the presentation.

## UNDERSTANDING WHY CUSTOMERS DON'T CLOSE

Now that we understand that closing the door in telephone sales is the only way to make sales, it is imperative that we understand why customers <u>don't</u> close over the telephone. I find it critical that before learning how to close, TSRs develop an understanding as to why customers refuse to be closed. Clearly, there is a rhyme and a reason to the madness. In fact, there are seven reasons why customers don't close over the telephone:

1. **Afraid to Commit Over the Telephone**

   Because customers can't see the TSR or the product, and because the telephone sales industry has such a lousy reputation, many customers are afraid to commit when speaking over the telephone. They would rather have the TSR "send something in the mail," or "come on out with documentation," where they can grasp the offer with their own eyes.

2. **Don't Understand the Offer**

   Many customers would be valuable buyers if they only understood exactly what the offer entailed. When TSRs present a program poorly, it is not the fault of the customers that they don't understand the offer. In addition, each customer grasps the intricacies of even the simplest program in a different way. Without the customer saying "I don't understand the offer" and without the TSR asking "Do you understand the offer?" the telephone sales presentation is lost because of confusion and misunderstanding about the offer.

3. **No Money**

   This is the most common reason why customers object to closing a sale. One third of the time, the customer is telling the truth when he says he doesn't have the money to afford the product. If so, the TSR did a poor job of qualifying in the early stages of the presentation. That type of prospect should never have been presented the product. One third of the time, the customer is using "no money" as a brush off to allude the TSR. This brush off has worked so often in the past that society has conditioned customers to feign poverty. One third of the time, the customer is saying he has "no money" because, in his

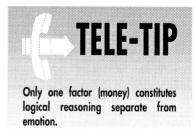

Only one factor (money) constitutes logical reasoning separate from emotion.

opinion, he doesn't have enough money to afford the product. At this stage, it is the TSR's job to demonstrate why in fact he does have enough money to close the sale.

## 4. No Need

As we have learned, customers will purchase a product only when the TSR can generate a need for the product. A lack of need is the paramount reason why most customers won't close a sale. No matter how much effort the TSR puts into the presentation, customers oftentimes feel that they have little need for the product, unless the TSR establishes a path between product and the customers (For example, the TSR must prove to the customer that he needs a couch, and the TSR must establish the reasons why the customer needs it).

## 5. No Want or Value

Similar to the need category, this is a difficult objection to overcome. Customers don't close because they don't have the <u>desire</u> to do so. Perhaps they don't want to close, or perhaps they don't value the product being offered so they don't have an incentive to close. In any event, getting inside customers and probing their minds is a difficult proposition even for the most skilled TSR. Even if the telephone sales presentation is flawless, there are a certain percentage of customers who just won't close until the TSR can establish a relationship between what the customer wants or values and what the product delivers.

## 6. No Hurry

Often, customers don't feel any incentive to close a sale over the phone because they recognize the fact that time is on their side. Unless the TSR can convey that the customer must have the product NOW, the customer is not going to feel that there is any urgency to complete the sale. TSRs always have the difficult dilemma of motivating the customer to make a decision today, instead of procrastinating until another day.

## 7. No Trust

TSRs will never close over the telephone if they don't build trust between themselves, their customers and their products. In such a case, customers may not be afraid to commit to a product over the telephone – just afraid to commit to <u>this</u>

product over the telephone, because they don't feel a common bond that breeds comfort and trust. If there isn't a line of trust between customer and TSR, the customer will never close.

Six of these seven reasons are personal "feel" reasons that have little to do with outside factors (Afraid to commit, Don't understand, No need, No want or value, No hurry, No trust). They center upon how a person feels at the moment he is called, and what that person believes about what he is hearing. Only one factor (money) constitutes logical reasoning separate from emotions. And even in this case, money is a very emotional subject and emotions often shape the way people behave with regard to it. If anything, this goes to demonstrate even more conclusively that closing customers over the telephone is an emotional game predicated upon selling pictures and appealing to feelings. The common theory that selling is a logical contest is quite incorrect.

## HOW TO OVERCOME CUSTOMERS' FEARS OF THE CLOSE

"It's not a big deal" is the phrase I tell my telephone sales representatives over and over again when teaching *them* how to close sales. "I know you can do it, because you've done it before." All TSRs go through valleys where they

**TELE-TIP**

Ask for the order, and don't give up.
Keep asking, in different ways.

believe that closing is a terrible ill that no sane individual can master. They consider closing such a dramatic act of telephone selling that the very thought stops them from making money. Experienced TSRs and rookies alike feel this way at one time or another, and that goes with the nature of the job. Under these circumstances, one thing is obvious: if I am having such a difficult time convincing my TSRs that closing is not a very big deal, how can my TSRs teach their customers that being closed for a sale is not that big of a deal?

Until the TSRs believe it themselves and overcome their fears of closing, they will have a difficult time convincing their customers that closing is no big deal.

Clearly, customers are afraid of the close because it is the customer who has to make a decision from which both the customer and TSR, not to mention the company that owns the product, will benefit. Thus, it's the TSR's job to reassure the customer that he is making the right choice. But what about the TSR who is absolutely petrified of closing for the sale? How can this TSR overcome this on behalf of himself, his product and his customer, and reassure the customer that accepting the close is the right thing to do?

Below are the reasons TSRs must become comfortable with the close, begin reassuring their customers, and make them comfortable too.

**TELE-TIP**

When TSRs present a program poorly, it is not the fault of the customers that they don't understand the offer.

- ## Closing is not slamming

  Slamming is a common word used in telephone call centers to represent the art of pushing through closes that customers don't want. For example, sending an order for children's books when the customer said "no" would be considered a "slam", and the TSR who commits this fraud is usually terminated on the spot. Too many TSRs have come to believe that ethical, professional closes are "slams," and they believe this for two reasons. First, because they read the newspapers and watch the television and are themselves conditioned that most telephone selling is fraudulent. Second, they have probably known peers in the telephone selling industry who did "slam." TSRs who believe that closing is slamming are wrong! TSRs must focus their minds and re-condition their intellects to comprehend that closing for the sale (i.e. asking the customer to make a decision) is not a slam at all. Instead, it is just another aspect of communication which motivates the customer to make a decision (as opposed to motivating him to answer a question, listen to a benefit, or provide an objection). In life, each one of us closes countless times every day. When TSRs analogize closing in life every day to closing over the telephone, they will begin to truly understand the difference between closing and slamming.

- ## Closing is only fair

  I spent some time with a TSR who couldn't quite understand why she should close over the phone. Her responses to me were "I don't want to be harsh," "I don't want to make them do something they don't want to do," etc. I agreed 100% with her philosophy of selling, because under no circumstances should a TSR want to force customers to act against their wishes. However, that's not what closing is about, and I finally was able to get this TSR to understand when I explained closing this way. "When you call the customer, you want to be honest and forthright with him, right? Then beating around the bush when you want the order isn't being forthright, and that's misleading. Why are you calling? To close the sale!! Selling the customer for hours without applying the close is really the worst thing you can do to that customer, isn't it? Isn't it more fair to the customer to admit that your primary objective is to earn a close, and that's what you are going to do?"

- ## Closing is what customers want TSRs to do

  The relationship between a TSR and customer is a lot like the relationship between a parent and child. Although the child acts as if he doesn't want guid-

**TELE-TIP**

Closing the customer and completing the sale is the reason a telephone sales presentation is delivered.

ance, it is in fact guidance that he truly desires. And although a parent usually doesn't want to force guidance upon a child in the fear that the child may begin to disrespect the parent, it is this very guidance which good parents provide to help their children grow. In the world of telephone selling, customers want to hear the TSR close. When the TSR closes, the customer sees that close as an outlet to end the conversation, because a close means a decision needs to be made. Perhaps the customer will try to end the conversation by agreeing to the close. Perhaps he will try to end the conversation by rushing off the telephone. In any event, many customers won't say this publicly, but they need guidance and motivation, and have very little problem accepting it.

- **Customers don't know a close from an opening**

Only professionals truly know and understand their own business. In 90% of all telephone sales presentations, the customer has absolutely no idea of the various stages the TSR is in while the TSR presents his program. Customers don't study introductions and benefits, trial closes and transition phrases. With that in mind, the TSR needs to view the close with as little apprehension as he would the introduction or qualification. The threat and danger of closing is always in the mind of the TSR.

Now that we understand why the TSR must become comfortable with the close, how can the TSR make his customer comfortable with the close?

- **Emphasize its insignificance**

The telephone sales representative has a huge advantage over the customer after he closes for the sale. The customer may hear a close and become overwhelmed with apprehension. Then, the TSR can come back and say "I understand that making a decision is a difficult process, but I want you to know that it's really not that big of a deal." The sentence "It's really not that big of a deal" is one of the best sentences a TSR can express to his customer. It takes away fear, lets customers understand that they need to reconsider any fear they have, and it brings head-on the conflict customers face when they attempt to make decisions over the telephone ( i.e. is buying over the telephone good or not?) A TSR can do little more than to meet the customer head-on with the statement "It's really not that big of a deal".

- **Provide peer examples**

I am constantly amazed at how peer pressure dominates the world we live in. Customers listening to a sales presentation over the telephone tend to become extremely comfortable with the close when they realize how many of their peers have participated in the program being sold. It's a fact that very few people enjoy doing things first, or doing things by themselves. Closing becomes fun when customers learn that saying "yes" puts them among friends.

> "I've already spoken to many of your neighbors, and they are very excited about this offer."

> "Presently, our product has been distributed to over 40,000 members in your city alone."

● **Illustrate why the close is beneficial**

When customers truly <u>desire</u> something special, they don't care how they receive it. If I were walking down the street and a pedestrian offered me ten million dollars to stand on my head naked in front of the White House, all I'd ask for was the space. Ten million dollars to me is beneficial! Customers become enamored with the TSR's close when they become enthusiastic about the product being offered. It is very rare for a customer interested in a product to be intimidated by the close. The objective for the TSR is to find benefits and features of the product that tie in specifically with the customer, and paint a picture of how the customer will be better off after purchasing the product.

> "You and I have been talking about why this offer is so good for you, and I think we both know it is. Let's get you started so you can have it by Monday."

● **Close often**

Much of what is written in this book derives its theory from customer conditioning, and the fact that customers are conditioned by those around them to act and react in certain ways (friends, media, sales people). Using conditioning as our concept, it is amazing how fast customers become conditioned to accept the close after they continue to hear it. Ask for the order, and don't give up. Keep asking in different ways.

## LEARNING WHEN TO FIND THE RIGHT TIME TO CLOSE

There are certain things in life that we all have to do for the first time: going to school on that first day, having a broken arm or leg for the first time, closing the sale for the first time. Unlike going to school or breaking an arm or leg, the TSR has the advantage of closing the sale for the first time, hundreds of times a day, for his entire career. This is because closing is always new to every one of the customers to whom the TSR presents the product, and because each customer is always new to the TSR. This is what makes closing an art, as it is different every time. This is also what keeps the job of a talented TSR exciting. Unfortunately, it is also what makes the job so difficult. The reality is that because closing is so difficult, and because the rejection rate is so high, it takes hours and hours of effort before proficiency begins to set in.

**The whole concept of closing over the telephone can be focused upon three techniques: TSRs must open doors at the beginning of the presentation. TSRs must encourage customers to go through doors in the middle of the presentation. TSRs must close doors at the end of the presentation.**

As the TSR begins the process of closing over the telephone, his goal should be to become talented at understanding *when* to close. *When*, as it relates to the timing of the closing, is more important to the telephone sales presentation and the close than *How* to properly close over the telephone. For example, here is why *how* is not that important when closing sales. <u>If a customer wants to say "yes" to a close because the TSR has done a wonderful job selling the product and motivating the customer, then no matter how the TSR goes into the close, the customer is going to say "yes".</u>

"Mr. Smith, I know you don't want this product, do you?"

"Of course I do. It sounds great. Sign me up."

*How* the TSR closes the sale doesn't matter as much, because if the customer really, truly is sold on a product (as a customer should be), then the close becomes a simple function that motivates a customer who has already been sold on the product to buy it. In ideal situations, the close is nothing more than a push; a boost and a force that motivates the customer to say "yes".

*When* the TSR closes the telephone sales presentation becomes the critical factor in closing, because very few customers are truly sold on any product at the end of the initial presentation. Sensing what the customer will do at various stages of the sales presentation and then taking advantage of this sense by understanding *when* to close will allow the TSR to complete a multitude of sales. For example, I believe that most customers who agree to a close would very often not agree to that very same type of close if it came either later or earlier in the telephone sales presentation. The timing of the close is that important. Many customers who refuse to close refuse to do so, not because of what they hear or don't hear, but because of the timing of when the TSR begins the telephone sales close. (Timing means everything. Perhaps the customer feels unsure all of a sudden, or has second thoughts, or perhaps the customer hears something that doesn't appeal to him.) Since the timing of the close makes all of the difference in a telephone sales presentation, here are nine steps to ensure that the TSR closes when it is the correct time to do so:

## 1. Close *when* needs and wants have been identified

Customers refuse to say "yes" to a close until they think that they need the product, or feel that they want the product. Before the TSR begins the close, he must do a thorough job of tying in either needs or wants (or both) so that the customer is compelled to agree to the close *when* the TSR delivers it. Once those needs or wants have been established, it's time to close! For example, the TSR may utilize a trial close question to establish agreement with a need or want, and follow that with a close:

*Trial Close*      "Ms. Jones, you and I agreed that you want a car that gets 40 miles or more to the gallon, didn't we?"

*Close*      "In that case, let's set a time for 2:00p.m. tomorrow so you can look at our new cars, okay?"

## 2. Close *when* the customer, not the TSR, values the product

Before they close, TSRs often fall into the trap of waiting and waiting for the customer to appreciate the product as much as the TSR does. This trap sinks TSRs all of the time. A golden rule for the TSR is that the customer is <u>not</u> required to value the product as much as the TSR does. Instead, the customer merely needs to value the product enough to buy it. Too often, TSRs continue to probe and trial close and sell benefits of the product with the hope that the customer will respond with the same enthusiasm or interest that the TSR has, and the TSR won't close until the customer responds appropriately. It must be recognized that customers will never respond with as much fervor as will TSRs. As soon as the customer demonstrates that he likes what he is hearing, the TSR should begin the closing process.

## 3. Close *when* the customer elicits buying signs

As we learned in the forward, the skills of listening and hearing are important throughout a telephone sales presentation. With that in mind, the TSR has a golden opportunity to understand *when* to close the sale, because he can utilize these skills to identify buying signs from the customer. Buying signs from the customer include:

"Now that is something my wife said she needed."

"Are you sure the books come in hard cover?"

"That is a very good point."

"Interesting."

"I never thought of that."

"Why?"

"How long have you been working with the company?"

"When did your company begin selling over the telephone?"

"I really wasn't prepared for anything like this today."

"I really should probably ask my wife before I do anything."

Whenever a customer expresses a buying sign, the TSR must pick up on that by hearing everything that is said and understanding what it means. Then, the TSR must use that buying sign as a springboard to close the sale.

## 4.　Close *when* the customer is silent

Silence means one of two things. Either the customer is thinking about the offer (which probably means that the customer is out of objections) or he is waiting for the TSR to go somewhere with the conversation, as the customer has relinquished control of it. If the customer is thinking about the offer, he is weighing whether or not to accept it. At this moment, the TSR should give the customer a little nudge forward by closing. On the other hand, if the customer is waiting for the TSR to lead him, then the customer is at the mercy of the TSR, and should be led to the close as well. So, when things become silent don't panic, because it's not necessarily a bad thing. It may simply be time to close.

## 5.　Close *when* the customer asks questions

The greatest stroke of luck for the TSR is when the customer asks questions. In contrast, when the customer provides objection after objection, the TSR knows that he needs to dig himself out of a ditch. By asking questions, the customer is letting the TSR know that he is very interested in what he is hearing. This is a golden opportunity for the TSR to answer the questions persuasively, and then close the customer on the answers.

## 6.　Close *when* the customer sounds excited

Timing a close is never more important than in this case. I once managed a TSR who was having what I thought was a perfect call. More than half way through the telephone sales presentation, the customer sounded excited with the product, and he and the TSR were getting along fabulously. I was monitoring in my office, and I kept screaming "Close the sale, close the sale!" At this point, the prospect wanted the program and there was no reason to continue with the presentation. If the TSR had closed at that time, the customer would have certainly agreed to the sale. Unfortunately, the TSR was enjoying himself far too much, maybe even more than the customer, and the telephone sales presentation continued another ten minutes. By that time, the customer had a mood swing, the TSR couldn't figure out why the customer wouldn't close, and the sale was missed. Hearing that the customer is excited should tell the TSR one thing: CLOSE!!!!!

## 7.　Close *when* the pace of the telephone presentation changes

Figuring out *when* to close becomes even more difficult when the pace of the telephone presentation begins to change. For example, if there is a nice, crisp conversation between TSR and customer and all of a sudden the customer becomes slow and methodical as if his attention is lost, the TSR is obligated to focus the customer back into the call. One of the best ways to do this is by closing for the sale.

### 8. Close *when* the customer objects, after a close

The best time to close is after the customer hears a close and objects. This is reminiscent of the fundamental philosophy of closing the sale, which states that the only way to close is to continually close. Every telephone sales trainer I have spoken with can recount hundreds of instances when the TSR closes, the customer objects to the close, the TSR responds to the objection and then gives up the sale as if it is a lost cause. Why doesn't the TSR respond to the objection and close again? For instance, if I (as the customer) have an issue and the TSR resolves my issue, then perhaps I have no more issues and I am ready to say "yes". I am a big believer that if the TSR makes a complete presentation and gets to the close, he should stay with the customer for as long as appropriate before giving up on the sales call. TSRs must recognize that closing once just isn't enough.

**TELE-TIP**

Even if the telephone sales presentation is flawless, there are a certain percentage of customers that just won't close until the TSR can establish a relationship between what the customer wants or values and what the product delivers.

### 9. Close *when* the customer agrees to benefits and features

In the chapter on benefits and features I emphasized the point that customers buy because of the benefits and features which motivate them to buy. In that regard, when the customer agrees with the TSR about one or many benefits and features, the customer is telling the TSR that it is a wonderful time to close for the sale, because the TSR has the credibility to close. Again, when to close is very much an issue of timing, and there is no better time to close for a sale than after the customer agrees with the TSR on various benefits and features.

## LEARNING *HOW* TO CLOSE

When I was considering becoming a high school basketball coach, I contacted one of my best friends who coached junior college basketball, and I asked him what he thought was the most important element of winning basketball games. Without hesitating, he said "You need to learn *how* to close in the final stages, otherwise you will never win." Although I never pursued a career coaching basketball, I did take what my friend said to heart, and I was able to transfer much of his philosophy to my training of telephone sales representatives.

I have spent a large portion of this chapter talking about the value in understanding *when* to close sales, and making sure that every reader recognizes that *when* is far more important than *how* when it comes to the closing cycle. What I would like to do now is demonstrate exactly where the *how* comes into play, because we cannot underestimate the importance of correctly learning *how* to close over the telephone. It is safe to say that all sales trainers agree that *how* the TSR closes over the telephone makes a huge impact on the success of the telephone sales call. Too many TSRs with too few skills lose sales because they don't know *how* to close properly. The lack of skills and knowledge only sets a TSR back in his pursuit of the close.

I think it's only appropriate to explore further what my friend was talking about. Basketball teams every day play wonderful games, only to lose in the closing minutes because they don't know *how* to put teams away. Some of the teams get cocky with big leads, and they can't finish because they lose focus. Other teams try so hard to win games that when it comes to closing another team out they get nervous and tentative. I remember a recent professional basketball game where a team led by so many points in the second half that they stopped playing hard, instead falling back on old habits. Before they knew it, their opponent had cut the lead in half, then into thirds, and then into single digits. The team that once had a big lead in the second half had to scramble to hold on to victory. It was clear to me that this team did not know *how* to put the game away at the end.

Closing a customer while selling over the telephone encompasses the exact same traits as does closing an opposition basketball team in the closing minutes. I, and every telephone sales trainer in America, have probably heard countless telephone sales presentations that didn't end up as sales because the

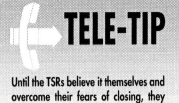

Until the TSRs believe it themselves and overcome their fears of closing, they will have a difficult time convincing their customers that closing is no big deal.

TSRs didn't understand exactly *how* to close the customers. TSRs who have had an easy presentation sometimes get too cocky, and they lose focus on their goals and objectives. Other TSRs try so hard to close sales that when it comes to closing a customer, they become nervous and tentative, and they lose self confidence. In any event, *how* the TSR closes can make all the difference.

It is mandatory that TSRs capture the fundamentals of closing if they are going to take that step forward and become successful. Both before a telephone call, and during the call, the TSR must begin thinking about the fundamentals of a successful telephone sales close. TSRs should begin thinking "What do I need to do in a particular situation?" "What is my client going to be looking for from my close?" Below are eight fundamental steps in learning *how* to close the customer for the sale:

## 1. Frame the close

When teaching *how* to close over the telephone, I teach my telephone sales representatives to frame the close around the areas of agreement between the customer and the TSR. Framing the close involves taking the aspects of the telephone sales presentation that the two parties agreed upon and focusing on those aspects utilizing benefits and features. There is no reason for the TSR to remind the customer about everything they had spoken about within the telephone sales presentation. The TSR should focus on framing the close with regard to the three or four truly positive issues both parties agreed upon.

> "We're both in agreement that buying children's books would contribute to your son's educational growth, and you do agree that the books are very fairly priced for their content. Let's get you started right away."

## 2. Don't change tone when closing

Too often (in the clutch) when one sentence can make or break a telephone sale, the TSR dramatically changes his tone, throwing both himself and the customer off guard. This may be intentional, because the TSR is trying to make a point, or it could be because, in the throes of the final moments, the TSR becomes nervous, causing his tone to change. As we touched upon earlier, the tone the TSR communicates over the telephone goes quite a distance toward building trust and confidence with the customer. TSRs who maintain a consistent tone put the customers in an extremely comfortable position. This comfortable situation makes a closing sentence sound less threatening and imposing.

## 3. Don't change pace when closing

More important than the tone of a conversation is the pace of the conversation. In nine out of ten instances, if the TSR speeds up the pace of his presentation at the close of the sale the sale will be lost. Speeding up the pace makes the customer believe the TSR is nervous and rushed, as if the TSR has another motive for trying to close the sale. It is imperative that the TSR maintain the same pace with which he started the conversation, especially when it is time to close the sale.

## 4. Close with empathy

TSRs need to remember that customers always recognize one important element of closing the sale. As in any relationship with two parties, customers want to feel cared about; as if the TSRs are looking out for their best interests. When a TSR closes with empathy, the customer is more apt to feel that the TSR is somebody who has earned the sale. (Often , the customer feels as if it is his sale to give away – and in fact it is!) In addition, it is much <u>easier</u> for a customer to agree to a sale when he feels the TSR has empathy for him. Not too many customers assist TSRs by agreeing to sales when the TSRs don't seem to care about the customers.

## 5. Be confident in product / customer / abilities

Confidence can make or break a sale. I could spend a full day in the classroom teaching TSRs the importance of maintaining confidence on the telephone.

There is no doubt that customers realize everything that is going on with TSRs, as this relates to their confidence in selling the product. The TSR must maintain confidence with regard to three things in order to successfully close the sale:

Product

Customer

Abilities

### 6. Don't stumble, bumble or become somebody different

Smoothness and consistency during the close will always differentiate the successful TSR from the mediocre TSR. Because of the pressure closing causes, many TSRs stumble and bumble their way through the close, causing the customer to become uncomfortable. Every mannerism and trait that the TSR perfected throughout his sales presentation must remain the same during the close. A stumble here, or a bumble there, will alert the customer to the fact that a threatening decision is at hand.

### 7. Don't sound eager and anxious

Has a TSR who sounded eager ever come away with a sale? Absolutely, because he was able to transfer that eagerness into enthusiasm and excitement. But how many TSRs aren't able to transfer that eagerness into enthusiasm and excitement? Too many! The TSR must not *desire* the sale so much that he turns his customer off. In society, we can see plenty of examples where one person has been so eager and anxious for something that he turned another person off; a person who in a different context may have been interested in the offer after all.

### 8. Don't over-close by talking, talking, talking

The best TSRs know when to SHUT UP! TSRs who lack internal confidence and serenity find themselves talking on and on and on because they never quite feel that the customer understands what they are saying. This will always result in over-closing, which we have learned will result in lost sales. If a customer is ready and the TSR is persuasive, one sentence can provide just as strong a closing as four paragraphs.

In addition to the eight fundamental steps, here is a hint that many TSRs never learn about when it comes to closing over the telephone: <u>TSRs must recognize that identifying is the key to managing the telephone sales close</u>. Identifying when to close, identifying how to close and identifying the correct traits of the close all play an enormous role. For example, the TSR needs to identify when the timing is correct. In addition, the TSR needs to identify what he thinks the customer will say when he initiates the close. Identification also takes place when the TSR identifies which close he believes will properly do the trick and motivate the customer to agree to the sale. Furthermore, the TSR has to identify where in the sales cycle the telephone sales presentation rests. To illustrate, imagine a whole presentation coming to the very end. Did the TSR express enough benefits and features? Did the customer accept those benefits and features, or does he remain skeptical? Did the TSR probe the customer and establish his needs and wants, so that the customer is convinced that the TSR has sold him exactly the right product?

**TELE-TIP**

TSRs must focus their minds and recondition their intellects to comprehend that closing for the sale is not a slam at all. Instead, it is just another aspect of communication that motivates the customer to make a decision.

In telephone selling, much of this game must be played without the benefit of the basics which most outside sales representatives can utilize. This always makes identifying more difficult. These basics include the areas we have touched upon in other chapters, such as eye contact and physical proximity. Over the telephone, the TSR's greatest sales closes are motivated by the TSR's clearest sense of identification, without the clues outside sales representatives may rely upon.

## TWO ELEMENTS THAT MOTIVATE CUSTOMERS TO CLOSE

Closing is an art form that has a great deal to do with psychology. With this in mind, I have spent some time trying to figure out exactly what motivates a customer to accept a close. Is it persistence? Aggressiveness? Glitz? Begging? Certainly, on any given telephone call the above may work, although not in any high percentage of the time. In essence, there are millions of traits, expressions and styles that motivate customers to close: voice, tone, pace, melody and inflection, trust, credibility, relationship- building, rapport. With this in mind, below are the two elements that I believe most motivate customers to close over the telephone:

1. **Time**

   It is most fascinating to recognize that "time" is quite the motivating factor when closing sales. When customers feel that the time is right, they act. The TSR must create the sense of urgency that the time is right. Asking questions that utilize time, and framing the close around this sense of urgency makes customers buy.

   > "If you have my product and your competitor doesn't, you win and he loses. If your competitor has my product and you don't, he wins and you lose. Don't you agree it's time to get this product before your competition does?"

   Customers don't want to feel that they are being rushed, yet at the same time they want to be told when they are missing out. When they are told they need to act, they often do just that. Think of the time factor for a moment. Department store chains have discounts and sales events wrapped around time parameters (48 hour sale, etc.). Time factors may spur a customer to act.

## 2. Information

Customers begin to form a desire for something when they feel that the item can provide them with constructive and valuable information. Many telephone sales come simply from the customers' desire for information. TSRs must frame the close around their product's ability to provide beneficial information to the customer.

> "As we talked about, our children's books are packed with more information than your child could ever hope to assimilate – and it is information that will help your child in school. Let's get you started."

## EFFECTIVE TELEPHONE CLOSES THAT SHUT THE DOOR

In the following few pages, I illustrate a number of different closing techniques which will assist the TSR when it comes time to close the customer over the telephone. It is my opinion that closing the door in person and closing the door over the telephone involve 90% of the same theories, with a few differences in each venue. There are many areas of crossover. However, the important thing to remember in telephone selling is that the objective the TSR is trying to reach prior to closing over the telephone is an objective which involves timing and picture painting, both of which we have explored in detail. Perhaps timing is the most critical avenue prior to closing over the telephone. Is the customer ready? Is the TSR ready? So when utilizing these, or any telephone closes, it is mandatory that the TSR use these closes in conjunction with the theories of timing and picture painting. Is it the correct time to try a close? Can I paint a picture of my product and tie it successfully into a close?

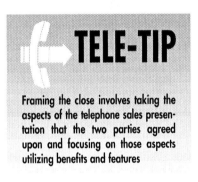

**TELE-TIP**

Framing the close involves taking the aspects of the telephone sales presentation that the two parties agreed upon and focusing on those aspects utilizing benefits and features

### Address close

"I see your address is 1234, is that correct?"

"Let's get you started. Are you still on Wilkinson Way?"

"We can get you started, I simply need to confirm your mailing address…"

### Let me make a note of that close

"That sounds wonderful. Let me make a note that when you purchase, you want to purchase ten gallons."

"Let me write that down so I will remember it when we fill out the application."

"Is that something I should keep in mind when we begin the process of enrolling you?"

### Ben Franklin close

"Let's review what we have talked about. You mentioned quality was important to you, and we both agreed that my program offers you quality, right? And, we agreed that price is important, and we both came to the conclusion that my product is competitive when it comes to price. Since we agree on so much, let's schedule a date, okay?"

### "If I , will you" close

"If I provide you with everything you want, will you join us for 60 days?"

"If I can show you a way you can increase production and decrease expenses, will you be interested in meeting with me at 3:00pm on Thursday?"

### Double question close

"You like your product delivered on Thursdays, correct? And you like deliveries twice a month, right? Let's get you started."

### Peer pressure / credible history close

"Over two thirds of all your competitors have joined our program. Can we start you today?"

"If I can provide you with phone numbers of your peers who have accepted our offer, will you join us next week?"

### Money close

"Will you be paying by check, cash or credit card?"

### "What would you have done" close

"Obviously, I didn't do a great job selling because you are still not interested. Let me ask you, what would you have done if you were in my shoes?"

### "Better – not the same – but better" close

"If I can demonstrate to you that we have something better – not merely the same – but better, would you be interested in hearing about it?"

### Choice Close

"I have Saturday at 4:00 p.m. and Saturday at 2:00 p.m. available, which is better?"

## ONE LINER CLOSES

"Okay?"

"Let's do it!"

"We can do this for you right now…"

Is there any reason why we can't get together on this right now?"

"Will what you mentioned make the difference between
a 'yes' and a 'no'?"

"Sound good?"

"So there isn't any reason why you wouldn't want to
get started today, is there?"

"Do you have any questions?"

"After all that we've discussed, do you have any more questions?
Good, I have you down as…"

"Any reason why you would want to wait?"

"Don't you agree that everyone will benefit by starting today?"

"Sooner the better, right?"

"Isn't it time to get this going?"

"It's time we made a decision, don't you agree."

"Alright?"

## COEN'S CENTERPIECE TO CLOSING SPECIFIC STEPS TO CLOSING IN THE TELEPHONE SALES CYCLE

Generate Agreement On Specific Benefits And Features

Create Enthusiasm About The Offer

Hear Buying Signals And Encourage The Customer To Understand Their Own Signals

Understand The Pace And Timing Of The Presentation

Uncover What The Customer Wants And / Or What The Customer Needs

Establish A Special Relationship Which Encourages Credibility

Establish And Sustain Control Of The Direction Of The Presentation

Handle Objections Succinctly / Overcome Objections Persuasively

Ask For The Order

# CHAPTER 10

## TRANSITION PHRASES

An element of telephone selling we have touched upon briefly in previous chapters is a component that doesn't receive very much attention around telephone sales training rooms. This component involves using <u>transition phrases</u> in communication with customers when handling an objection or question or statement from a customer. Why transition phrases have not become an everyday sales tool in sales training rooms is a mystery to me. I have always considered transition phrases a valuable tool when selling over the telephone, because transition phrases are aspects of communications that often mean the difference between calming a customer's concerns and answering his questions, or losing a customer's confidence and the sale as well.

I train TSRs to view transition phrases as the first step in responding to a customer after he expresses an objection, question or statement. Hence, a transition phrase is a sentence or two designed to facilitate trust, confidence, conversation, empathy, sincerity, smoothness and cohesiveness between the TSR and the customer. Transition phrases assist the conversation by designing responses for the TSR that flow freely. In addition, transition phrases are effective because the TSR can utilize them to begin the process of persuading, convincing and selling the customer on the TSR's primary objective.

The most popular and often used transition phrase when handling an objection is:

> "I understand exactly how you feel."

The most popular and often used transition phrase when answering a question is:

> "That's a very good question, and I'm glad you asked."

The most popular and often used transition phrase when handling a statement is:

> "I'm very happy you brought that up."

**TELE-TIP**

Transition phrases assist the conversation by designing responses for the TSR that flow freely.

It is important to recognize that there is no successful alternative to using transition phrases, so I believe it is extremely important to train TSRs to utilize transition phrases well. Customers lose interest in the conversation very quickly when the TSR counters with a response that completely ignores much of what the customer cares about. This is one of the critical dangers when handling customer questions, objections and statements without utilizing a transition phrase. If customers don't feel comfortable, if they feel alienated, if they feel unsure about the nature of the conversation, they will be more apt to refuse to become involved. Utilizing a casual and confident transition phrase separates earning a customer's trust from losing it.

Transition phrases solve this problem by allowing the customer to feel comfortable while the TSR begins refuting that customer's points. Customer comfort is a primary objective when handling an objection, question or statement. To provide an analogy, try to remember back to a conversation on the telephone or in person when the conversation didn't fare well. In this ill-fated conversation, transition phrases probably were never utilized, and if they were, they were likely not utilized properly. Why? Because each party was too busy trying to force their opinions across, without spending the time to make the other person feel comfortable. When the TSR doesn't utilize transition phrases, the customer and TSR tend to have a stilted and uncomfortable argument. If the TSR spends too much time trying to force his argument across to the customer, the customer is going to feel exactly as most people would – forced, coerced and threatened.

> TSR:        "I want you to buy the program because it will help you out a great deal."
>
> CUSTOMER:  "I don't think it will help me out, so I'm going to pass this time around."
>
> TSR:        "You're wrong. It will help you, because it's everything you're looking for."
>
> CUSTOMER:  "I appreciate the offer, but I'm not interested."
>
> TSR:        "I totally disagree with you. Our product is great."

Notice, the TSR never includes a transition phrase when beginning his rebuttal. Obviously, that lack of a transition phrase damages the TSR in his attempts to sell the customer. With a transition phrase, the customer will be more apt to hear everything else the TSR wants to say. In the example above, in each rebuttal, the TSR attempts to force his point upon the customer without taking any interest in the customer's opinions or complaints. How does the customer feel about having all his thoughts and con-

**TELE-TIP**

Once the customer feels that the TSR is on his side, the TSR needs to begin making one point after another to slowly change the customer's mindset.

cerns ignored? In the above example, the TSR is too busy worrying about what he wants, and the TSR is not spending enough time making sure the customer feels satisfied with the conversation.

TSR: "I believe you should purchase the program because it will help you out a great deal."

CUSTOMER: "I don't think it will help me out, so I'm going to pass this time around."

TSR: "I understand how you feel, and I want you to know that we are not asking for a decision if you're not completely comfortable making one."

CUSTOMER: "I appreciate the offer, but I'm not interested."

TSR: "That makes sense. Mr. Smith, I want you to be reassured that my main objective is not to obligate you to make a decision right now. May I ask, what parts of the program are you not interested in right now?"

As we have explored in the past, *what* the TSR says is an extremely valuable component to the telephone sales presentation. Considering that transition phrases are the first sentence or two a customer hears after a customer rejects, objects, makes a statement or asks a question, it is extremely significant that the customer hears a well thought out, relaxed, confident sentence that encourages him to want to hear more.

## TRANSITION WORDS THAT BEGIN A FIRST SENTENCE

I understand

I know exactly

I hear

I feel

Good point

In the past

That makes good sense

I'm glad

I agree

You are absolutely

## TRANSITION WORDS THAT COMPLEMENT A FIRST SENTENCE

However

Moreover

On the other hand

But

Once you see

Yet

Still

Nevertheless

Furthermore

Besides

Fortunately

In fact

At the same time

## HOW TO UTILIZE TRANSITION PHRASES SUCCESSFULLY

Transition phrases should encompass the following fundamentals:

### Begin The Rebuttal
Transition phrases are the first sentence a customer should hear after the customer objects, makes a statement, or asks a question.

### Be Empathetic Of The Customer's Position

Customers should feel that the TSR is involved with their feelings. The TSR's response should not only be empathetic, but it should also convey a message of simple understanding.

### Agree With The Customer's Position

If the TSR's first response is to negate everything the customer has said, the TSR will lose. If the TSR attempts to sound empathetic but then begins dismantling the customer's responses, the TSR will lose. The TSR must agree with what the customer says, in a way that lets the customer feel that he is right for the moment.

### Direct The Call Slowly To The TSR's Position

Once the customer feels that the TSR is on his side, the TSR needs to begin making one point after another to slowly change the customer's mindset.

### Only One Or Two Sentences

A transition phrase is merely a sentence or two of preview, prior to the actual rebuttal portion of the presentation.

## EXAMPLES OF GENERAL TRANSITION PHRASES:

"I understand how you feel, because other customers have felt the same way."

"I know exactly how you feel. Moreover, I can relate. Fortunately, I haven't yet told you why you may want to reconsider."

"I agree with everything you are saying. They are good points. However, I think once you explore the pluses and features of our program, you will be extremely happy."

"Mr._____, I hear why you are objecting, but I don't want you to think that our program is so specific. Furthermore, it wouldn't be fair to you if I didn't explain the rest of the program."

"You are making perfect sense, Mr._____ . In fact, when I first began familiarizing myself with this product, I felt quite the same way."

"The good news is that you are not the first person who has felt this way, so don't think you are alone. At the same time, here is why I think you might change your mind."

"That's a good question, because other customers I talked with have felt the same way initially. I can't figure out if I'm not explaining the program well, so give me a moment to illustrate the facts."

"Your question brings up some valid issues, Ms. _____ . These are some of the more common issues I must deal with, because they mean  so much to our customers."

"That makes good sense to me, so I am not going to disagree with you.

I would like to show you exactly why there are far more benefits than just that one, however."

"In the past, that has often been true. Fortunately, the past is the past, and I think you will be quite happy with what we have today."

"I'm glad you asked that question. So many customers have approached me with the same question that I know it is a valid concern."

"Good point Mr._____ . Perhaps I should ask you a question or two to find out if I have an offer you are interested in. Tell me,…"

---

### THE CHILDREN'S BOOKS SELLING EXAMPLE

"At first glance, that tends to be true Ms._____ . However, once you see the beautiful illustrations, you will find out that they are professionally crafted."

"In the past, that was true. With today's modern style, however, each book is written for specific age groups."

"I understand exactly how you feel, because it is impossible for you to see the books today. Which matters most to you, quality stories or illustrations?"

"I'm glad you asked that question, because I want you to be comfortable with your decision."

"That's a good question. I've heard it before because other customers have felt the same way."

---

# CHAPTER 11

## HANDLING OBJECTIONS

Objections, objections, objections. Telephone objections appear to be overwhelming, don't they? TSRs feel as if objections are all they hear throughout a telephone sales presentation, and in many respects they are right. I recall one TSR who looked at me every morning with a pained look in his eyes. One day he told me "Dan, every time I come in, I need to take fifteen minutes to prepare myself for one 'NO' after another." Objections dominate the telephone sales presentation and they are extremely challenging to handle, much less overcome. What's a TSR to do with all these objections? It's quite a question.

TSRs must recognize that the dirt on objections is quite dirty: <u>Objections are as much a part of the everyday telephone sales cycle as sitting down and dialing the telephone</u>. Nothing extraordinary to report. As much as we wish it weren't the case, facts are facts: almost every telephone sales presentation includes objections, and usually a lot of them. Objections simply happen. Objections from customers usually are painful, appear to be irrational and are plain dangerous to the sales cycle, because they come so often and can be so challenging that they may cause a TSR to hit a wall, become exasperated, and stop the selling process. The objective of this chapter is to figure out exactly *how* to make objections less challenging and more beneficial, and how to both handle objections and overcome objections.

To handle and overcome objections, it's important to recognize that objections from the customer are not all "bad". The TSR may think objections are all bad, and they certainly feel that they are all bad, and this is a natural reaction, especially because objections are one of the aspects of the job that very often petrifies a TSR.

The reality, however, is that objections are far from being "bad". In fact, most customers object because they want to be sold and haven't heard the golden phrase that will sell them. If this is bad, I don't want to see good! When TSRs hear an objection, they immediately should think "Oh, I haven't told you what you need yet. Fair enough."

**Objections are as much a part as the everyday telephone sales cycle as sitting down and dialing the telephone.**

Indeed, customers understand that objections scare TSRs, and TSRs understand this point too. It tends to be those TSRs who don't demonstrate fear after an objection takes place who usually come out on top. There are other reasons customers object as well. Perhaps they truly don't like what they have heard to that point. Perhaps, customers object just because it seems like the thing to do. Since objections occur on almost every call, I train my TSRs to look out for customers who don't object. Those are the customers most likely to have just hung up the phone in the ear of the telephone sales representative.

Telephone selling would be too easy if customers were too agreeable, and the game isn't played that way. Hence, when objections take place in a telephone presentation, the TSR should be thinking along the following lines:

"Thank you for showing me the way…"

"I'm glad you are interested enough to stay on the phone…"

"I'm glad you want to tell me what I am doing wrong, so I can do right…"

"I am glad you are doing everything you can do to
help me make the sale…"

"I want you to keep objecting until you are motivated to buy –
then, I want you to stop objecting and say 'yes'…"

### *WHY* CUSTOMERS OBJECT

Aside from the basic built-in reason for a customer's objection – that he feels he <u>should</u> object-there are eight common reasons why customers offer objections.

1. **They Are Afraid**

   Many times customers are interested in what they are hearing, but they don't have the confidence and trust that doing business over the telephone is credible.

2. **They Don't Understand**

   This is a common reason why customers object. They don't want to admit that they aren't following the presentation, but their lack of understanding forces them to say "no".

3. **They Don't Want The Item**

   All of the psychology in the world won't correct the fact that many times customers are unimpressed, or under motivated, to purchase the product being offered.

### 4. They Don't Qualify

This issue is a sign that the TSR isn't doing his job. Before any presentation takes place, it is required that the TSR qualify the customer to make sure the customer is eligible to hear the presentation.

### 5. The Price Is Too High

Price is often referred to as the most difficult objection to overcome. When the customer insists that the price is too high, the TSR must establish value in his product to substantiate credibility with the price. In many instances, the customer just can't afford the price, and even establishing value falls on deaf ears.

### 6. The Price Is An Automatic Excuse

Price is the first objection a customer uses when he doesn't have a reason to object, because customers have learned that price is a very difficult objection for TSRs to overcome.

### 7. Societal Conditioning

Society has conditioned customers to provide objections, based on the assumption that any conversation on the phone isn't worth the customer's time and effort.

### 8. They Need More Information

Does the customer trust the TSR? Does the customer feel he is ready to make a decision? In most instances, customers object by requesting written information that they may peruse at their own pace.

Finding out why customers object is the main ingredient for dealing with objections. TSRs often say "I've studied this product for two weeks and I know this is the best product to own!! Why can't my customer understand this?" and the frustration the TSR has with his customer is palatable. Through it all, TSRs must be cognizant of the fact that customers have their reasons, and whether those reasons are right or wrong has no bearing on the presentation.

## STEPS TOWARD HANDLING AND OVERCOMING OBJECTIONS

As you can see, customers always have a reason for objecting. The challenge for the TSR is to uncover the reason and then deal with the objection. Herein lies the rub. How does the TSR change the customer's thinking without overstepping boundaries and creating negative friction? Most of the time, explaining to a customer why he is wrong to object will only strengthen his thoughts that he was right. When told they are wrong, customers think "How can a stranger whom I have never met and will never even see convince me that he is right and I am wrong?"

Below are the ways a TSR can convince customers that their objections may not be right:

- **Don't Try To Convince Them They May Not Be Right**

    Trying to convince customers they may not be right when they object will never work, because this opens up an adversarial relationship between the TSR and customer. Empathizing with the customer's statements by utilizing a sincere transition phrase is the first step toward overcoming an objection.

    "I understand how you feel…"

    "That makes perfect sense, Ms. Smith…"

    "Mr. Jones, that is very interesting…"

    "I hear exactly what you are saying…"

    "I recognize your concerns, and I'd like to address them carefully…"

    "Let me reassure you Mr. Jones, you are not the first customer who has felt this way…"

    "Mr. Jones, I and everybody I have talked with can relate to exactly what you are saying…"

- **Utilize Superior Listening Skills**

    If the customer feels that what he is saying matters to the TSR, then the customer will be more likely to continue expressing his views. By utilizing superior listening skills the TSR is creating a relationship between the customer and TSR that encourages such expression. While the customer senses that his comments are earning a response, the TSR is forging a trust with the customer so that when the TSR responds, the customer will pay attention.

- **Plant Seeds In Their Minds**

    Provide one or two simple benefits of the program that don't threaten a customer's opinion, but instead show the customer that additional views exist. Planting seeds can be accomplished by performing verbal nods; by selling very simple and non-threatening benefits, and by being patient.

- **Begin To Convince The Customer That Everybody Is On The Same Page**

    Changing his opinion becomes easier for the customer when he thinks that he came up with the belief. Ask questions which tie in the benefits that were sold in order to persuade the customer to come to a different point of view.

- **Ask Questions to Identify Why They Are Objecting**

    Many customers object for a reason, but they are not articulate enough to convey those reasons to the TSR. Do the reasons exist? Yes. Will the customer tell the TSR the reasons? No. Can the TSR find out the reasons? Yes. Simple questions are easiest, because simple questions invite simple answers, which can then be used by the TSR to formulate reasons why the customer is objecting.

"May I ask why?"

"Why are you not satisfied?"

"What can I do?"

"You must have a reason for saying that…may I ask what that is?"

"I know you're not interested…but isn't it true that_____is most important to you?"

"What makes you believe that?"

"Do you feel that way because of what you have heard?"

## ● Ask Questions To Identify Needs and Wants

One of the customer's primary reasons for stating an objection may be that the TSR has not developed a "needs base" with the customer. Usually, customers object because they don't feel their needs or wants have been met, and this is a valid objection from the customer's perception, because it is an honest objection.

It is important to recognize that objections from customers are not all bad.

Often, asking a simple question after the customer objects will allow the TSR to discover the customer's needs and wants. When the customer says "I'm just not interested," the TSR can answer with "May I ask why that is?" When the customer describes his needs, the TSR should take those needs and demonstrate how he can fulfill them. The needs base is perhaps the heart of a sale. An offer may sound fantastic and credible and sincere, but if there is no "need", there is no sale.

"Mr. Smith, what do you need from my product?"

"What are your three major desires when it comes to health care?"

"Do you want fried foods on Friday or Saturday? Why?"

## ● Ask Them to Elaborate More on Their Objections

Just because a customer provides an objection doesn't mean that he has expressed all of his concerns about that objection. In fact, customers often provide more information about an objection after making the objection than during the objection. The TSR must prod the customer to express more information about his objections. In the process, the customer will utter phrases, needs and information that can help the TSR better handle the original objection.

"It's interesting that you brought that up, Mr. Smith. How come you feel that way?"

"Why do you say that?"

"Did you feel this way before I called you this morning?"

● **Hear Each Answer Completely**

Asking questions amounts to very little if the TSR isn't hearing each answer completely. If the TSR doesn't hear exactly what the customer is saying, the TSR will lose a grand opportunity to discover which benefits, features and additional questions may be used to handle and overcome the customer's objections and eventually close the sale.

● **Sell Benefits and Features**

Because benefits and features sell products, the only way to handle and overcome objections is to sell benefits and features. If a prospect objects to purchasing children's books because the books are too expensive, and the TSR explains four or five benefits and features that sell the customer on forgetting about his objection, it is benefits and features that are making the difference .

> "I understand that you feel our product doesn't last as long as
> your present product. However,….."

> "What you will find fascinating about our product,…"

● **Trial Close**

After the above steps have been accomplished, the TSR can utilize a trial close to see how much success has been achieved. As we have learned, the trial close is used to both gain commitments from the customer and to find out if the TSR is on the right path. If the customer provides another objection, the TSR needs to begin the process over again by handling that objection. If the customer begins to agree with the TSR's views, then the TSR needs to solidify that agreement and move the sales cycle to the next level. In any event, it is mandatory that the TSR utilize the trial close at this stage, to make sure the customer and TSR are on the right page.

> "Would you agree that my program meets all of your criteria?"

> "Did you feel before our conversation that this product
> offered that much value?"

> "When comparing this offer to others, you feel more confident, don't you?"

---

### THE CHILDREN'S BOOKS SELLING EXAMPLE

*Customer: "I'm not interested in your children's books, because I can get the same books in the store."*

"I can understand why you feel that way, Mr. Smith, because each of my customers initially felt exactly the same way. I think you would be pleased to know that these books were commissioned by our company to be sold only over the telephone. Can you see why books commissioned to be sold only by telephone may provide a different view for your child than would those purchased in the store?"

"I recognize your concerns, and I'd like to address them carefully because they make quite a bit of sense. First, it's very important to recognize that our books are only available through this telephone offer, and that means there is an enhanced value to them. Not everybody can get these."

*Customer: "My child gets all the books he needs from the library."*

"Mr. Jones, I and everybody I have talked with can relate to exactly what you are saying. The library is a fantastic supplier of great books. These children's books aren't meant to replace his library reading, but in fact to complement it. May I ask, how often do you and your child visit the library?"

"Fantastic! That's exactly one of the reasons why I called. We are trying to chat with those parents who believe in reading and who use the library often. Tell me a little bit about your local library. Do you find its selection of books meet your child's needs?"

## "FEEL, FELT, FOUND"

The ability to handle objection is a science on which we could spend a whole book because it constitutes everything that we are taught not to do when growing up in society. This is a terribly difficult thing new telephone sales reps need to get past. For example, whereas we are taught in our private lives to say "okay" and stop after being objected to, we are taught in telephone sales to keep asking for the order, never accept a "no," and keep on pursuing. This concept is a difficult one for new and existing TSRs to accept.

In order to simplify the handling of objection, below I demonstrate a generic rebuttal to a generic early objection. The purpose of this is to teach one of the oldest sales responses in the world. First, read this sales rebuttal a few times and try to figure out the science behind it. Then read on to learn one of the oldest techniques in sales.

"Ms. Smith, I hear exactly what you are saying, and I often hear from customers who feel the same way. One of the nice things about my program is that customers feel it is very simple to understand, and as customers come to realize how it does save a lot of troubles down the line, they tend to enjoy it. Let me continue..."

This is an example of the "Feel, Felt, Found" sales formula, one of the more traditional and oldest sales formulas in the world. Designed to provide an easy transition after a customer objects, the goal in the "Feel, Felt, Found" formula is to:

*Feel* what the customer is saying.
Empathize and hear what he is expressing.

Express to the customer that he is not alone. Let him know that
many customers who have said "yes" to the offer also
*felt* the same way at one time.

Let the customer know what other customers have *found*;
i.e. the benefits of the program.

Customers feel comfortable and relaxed when they hear "Feel, Felt, Found".

Why does it work?

● **Customers need to feel like the TSR is listening to them**

They don't want to feel like what they are saying makes no sense. Thus, always start a rebuttal by letting them know the TSR is hearing what they are saying. (*"Ms. Smith, I hear exactly what you are saying…"*)

● **Customers need to feel like they are right**

Any time the TSR tells a customer that he is wrong, he will lose the sale. Customers are tenuous specimens, and they don't feel comfortable hearing that what they believe is wrong. None of us do. In this respect, it is important that the TSR tell customers that they are right, and casually let them know that they are not alone; they hold a very popular view . (*"…I often hear customers who feel the same way…"*)

● **Customers need to hear balanced and well thought out communication**

It is very difficult to communicate effectively with somebody who doesn't communicate well. As telephone sales professionals, this is our job; to communicate with folks who can't communicate well. If we put a customer in the position of not being able to communicate with us, then we pretty much give up the sale. The "feel, felt, found" approach ensures that the customers will hear an extremely smooth and well developed response to objections. It ensures that customers won't end sales calls because they don't have confidence in the TSRs sincerity and knowledge.

● **Make Sure Customers Understand Why Peers Had the Same Perception and Changed Their Minds**

So often, customers want to know that they are not alone. They want to know that if they say "yes" or agree to the offer, they aren't the first people to have done so. By ending the transition phrase with a reassuring benefit as to why other customers felt the same way and changed their minds, the TSR is setting the customer up with "reasonable doubt" – the idea that if somebody else objected and eventually agreed, maybe it's okay for them to do the same thing.

## WANTS AND NEEDS:
## THEIR RELATIONSHIP TO OVERCOMING OBJECTIONS

It takes literally hours and hours of practice for TSRs to learn the little tidbits and strategies of handling and overcoming objection. In this book alone, we have seen countless styles and techniques. Certainly, nobody would say that handling and overcoming objection is easy. But what becomes very important to grasp is the notion that not everything which *can be* learned to handle and overcome objections *should be* applied all of the time. In the call center environment, common questions I hear from TSRs include something as benign as "Do I start off a sentence with 'this word' or 'that word?" My response is always the

Customers always have a reason for objecting. The challenge for the TSR is to uncover the reason and then deal with the objection.

same. "Because customers don't hear the words you use, it doesn't matter. You want to communicate the themes, images and concepts of what you are trying to say." Another question I receive is "How come what I'm saying isn't working? It worked already yesterday." My response for this is equally as brief. "What you are saying worked yesterday because it appealed to yesterday's customers. What you are saying today doesn't appeal to today's customers. Think of the big picture – images, themes and concepts appropriate to the customer today."

Although I have mentioned this before, it bears repeating. TSRs spend too much time worrying about the little things, and not enough time thinking about the big things which close sales, and it is always the big things that separate success from failure. The big picture that handles and overcomes objections includes:

Am I coming across in a *confident* manner today?

Do I have a *rapport* with the customer that is conducive to selling?

Am I *listening* to the customer and encouraging him to continue providing me with information?

Am I *hearing* what the customer is saying and responding succinctly?

Does the customer *believe* that my product and I are credible?

Do I have *control* of the conversation and
am I maintaining direction?

Am I trying to figure out what this
customer *wants and needs*?

By objecting to the presentation, customers are often asking TSRs to sell them something they either <u>want</u> or <u>need</u>, and they are assisting the TSR in his presentation by explaining that everything they have received so far is information which <u>will not</u> work. Although TSRs view a customer's objection as either rejection, unfounded, or insincere, it is usually none of the three. Objections are the customer's way of expressing the fact that he isn't happy because his <u>needs base</u> or his <u>wants base</u> has not been met by the TSR. In effect, hearing an objection over the telephone, any objection, can be interpreted to mean any of the following:

"I'm not interested because <u>I don't need</u> your offer."

"I'm not interested because <u>I don't think</u> I need your offer."

"I'm not interested because <u>I don't feel</u> I need your offer."

"I'm not interested because <u>I don't value</u> your offer."

"I'm not interested because I don't <u>want</u> your offer."

"I'm not interested because <u>I don't think</u> I want your offer."

"I'm not interested because <u>I don't feel</u> I want your offer."

## WANTS:
## CUSTOMERS HAVE THEM AND
## TSRs MUST OVERCOME THEM

In society, we are consistently overwhelmed by what we choose to <u>want</u>, and these <u>wants</u> dictate much of what we do on a daily basis. For example, I can recall a scene in the mall just two weeks ago when a mother had two young girls under eight years old with her, and both were attempting to persuade the mother that they deserved milkshakes before leaving the mall. The mother kept saying "No," and the girls kept chanting "But mom, we <u>want</u> milkshakes!" in a whining tone that clearly demanded attention. TSRs learn very quickly that the way to handle objections and eventually close for the sale is to work with the customer on establishing what his <u>wants</u> are. More to the point, TSRs have come to learn that the way to handle objections and eventually close for the sale is to create <u>wants</u> for the customer, or frame their presentations around existing <u>want</u>s. Psychology and society dictate that if TSRs can give customers what they <u>want</u>, customers generally give TSRs what they <u>want</u> as well.

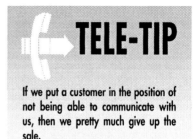

**TELE-TIP**

If we put a customer in the position of not being able to communicate with us, then we pretty much give up the sale.

Questions the TSR must pose to himself include "What does the customer <u>want</u>? How does this product tie into those <u>wants</u>? How can the TSR tie the product into those <u>wants</u>?" Discovering the customer's <u>wants</u> covers the emotional side of handling objections. We learned in a previous chapter that people are motivated by emotions and feelings far more than by logic and data. The objective for TSRs is to sell to a customer's emotions and feelings.

When it comes to telephone selling, the most precise definition of wants is:

### "Customer's desires"
Motivating customers to understand their desires, and proving to customers that these desires can be met through a product's benefits, features and facts

Telephone sales representatives don't use the <u>wants base</u> enough when selling over the telephone, and if they don't use the <u>wants base</u>, they will have a considerably difficult time motivating customers to understand and act upon their desires.

The reason that <u>wants</u> are so important is that they appeal to the emotional side of the customer, and tap into his reservoir of desire, while <u>needs</u> appeal to the customer's logic and tap into his reluctance. For example, I received a telephone sales call from a bank, and I had absolutely no <u>want</u> or desire for anything a bank might have to offer. I said "no" to the offer. Five minutes later, I received a telephone sales call about subscribing to a national baseball publication. In that case, I had an emotional interest and a <u>want</u> for more information. As the TSR began selling me on the baseball pennant races, I formed a desire. The TSR had pushed all of the correct buttons, and I was closed seconds later.

Emotion is always stronger than logic when it comes to convincing a customer to buy. I once knew a friend who had a mother who kept buying him irrelevant gadgets from a home shopping television network. Finally, my friend said "Mom, I don't <u>need</u> any of this stuff." His mom replied with "You're right, but I <u>want</u> to get you this stuff." Were there items being dis-

**TELE-TIP**

The "feel, felt, found" approach ensures that the customers will hear an extremely smooth and well developed response to objections.

played on this television channel that my friend might have <u>needed</u>? Certainly. Did his mom buy him any of those items? Absolutely not.

To break it down to its simplest form, if the customer <u>wants</u> the product, most of the time that customer will buy it. On the other hand, if the customer <u>needs</u> the product, quite often he may not buy it. Then again, if the TSR can demonstrate to the customer that he <u>wants</u> the product (emotions) and <u>needs</u> the product (data), the customer will very likely buy the product, and the TSR will experience success.

## NEEDS:
## THE SECOND PREREQUISITE TO
## OVERCOMING OBJECTIONS

In handling and overcoming objection, the stronger the TSR is in identifying which <u>needs</u> make the customer tick, the easier it will eventually be for the TSR to close the sale. What is a <u>needs base</u>? When it comes to telephone selling, the most precise definition of <u>needs base</u> is

### "Customers' requirements"
Motivating customers to understand their requirements, and proving to customers that these requirements can be met through a product's benefits, features and facts

<u>Needs</u> are not a mythical intangible that customers have and don't know about. Quite often, customers know exactly what their <u>needs</u> are. When handling objections, discovering a customer's <u>needs</u> involves reaching for the logical side of the customer. Then, the job of a good TSR is to ask appropriate questions to find out for himself what those needs are. If customers don't know what their <u>needs</u> are, it is even *more appropriate* for good TSRs to ask the right questions which will provide answers, not only for the TSRs, but for the customers as well.

Customers expect that TSRs will try to please them, and pleasing them is fulfilling their <u>needs</u> . Generally, discovering a customer's <u>needs</u> is the trick to handling his objection, but not always. If it were only that simple, there would be many more exceptional TSRs!!! The dilemma when discovering a customer's <u>needs</u> stems from the fact that customers are not always motivated by their <u>needs</u>. As we discussed above, a customer is more likely to be motivated by <u>wants</u> than by <u>needs</u>.

Let's think about this for a moment. How many of us, on a daily basis, find ourselves unmotivated by what we <u>need</u>. Probably quite a few of us. At the moment, I need an oil change, more milk, and a new light bulb for the corner lamp, but I am not motivated by any of those <u>needs</u>. In telephone selling, a major dilemma can arise when selling <u>needs</u>. What if the TSR establishes <u>needs</u>, sells the appropriate benefits and features conducive to the customer's <u>needs</u>, and still can't handle the customer's objections? What if the customer still isn't interested?

It's important to recognize that uncovering <u>needs</u> is not terribly difficult. In society, each and every one of us spends considerable time uncovering <u>needs</u> every day. Every time we ask a question of somebody (Are you hungry? How was your day at work? Why is the report not completed? What's new?) we are probing that person in order to discover <u>needs</u>.

### Questions Which Focus The Customer's Objections On <u>Wants</u> and <u>Needs</u>

"Obviously you have a reason for saying that, may I ask what that is?"

"May I ask why?"

"Can you tell me three things you need in a children's book that you presently don't have?"

"Is there something about these children's books that you feel won't benefit you?"

"May I ask what you like about our program?"

"If there is one thing you would be looking for in a program such as this, what would that be?"

"What do you think our program left out that you wish it had offered?"

"Please provide me with a few ideas on what you need that you presently are not getting."

What things do you need that you feel this program doesn't offer?"

"Mr. Smith, you explained to me that you need children's books that have written verbiage. What are the reasons you and your children want these books?"

"You told me you needed glossy style children's books. Do you value those glossy style books more or less than hardback ones? More than soft-back, or less?"

"I want to make sure that you truly understand my program. What makes you not want to take a look at this offer?"

"I understand exactly how you feel, however, have you ever given
any thought to the outstanding possibilities that go with
new and affordable insurance?"

"That makes perfect sense, Ms. Jones. The point I made is that by accepting
this offer, every pain, ache and illness can be treated that much faster, for
less money. Do you see how you can want something this exciting?"

Discovering a customer's <u>wants base</u> and <u>needs base</u> is fundamental to
handling and overcoming the customer's objections. Once the TSR has
established the customer's <u>wants</u> or <u>needs</u>, he can begin applying the benefits, features and facts of his program to the fulfillment of those <u>wants</u> and
<u>needs</u>. Tying in the benefits, features and facts of a program to a customer's
<u>wants base</u> and <u>needs base</u> will go a long way toward assisting the TSR in han-
dling a customer's objections.

## THE EIGHT MOST COMMON TELEPHONE OBJECTIONS, AND HOW TO HANDLE THEM SUCCESSFULLY

Below are the eight most common objections heard by telephone sales
representatives, along with the reasons they occur. Also included is a transition phrase for each objection, and a process to begin handling and overcoming the objection.

1. Objection #1:
   *"How can you guarantee that what you are telling me is true?"*

### Identify Why it Occurs

Over the past fifty years, society has conditioned people to believe only what they
see, not what they hear. That is where the term "I'll believe it when I see it" came
from, and that also explains why television has become such a controlling medium for both information and sales (Two of the largest cable networks are
news/information channels and home buying /shopping channels) . In fact, TSRs
will find quite often that customers demand nothing less than a fax or mail (visual) re-explaining an entire offer, even after they have heard that same offer from
a live TSR.

### Transition Phrase

"Ms Smith, I completely understand your concern."

### Handling and Overcoming The Objection

"Many other customers have said the exact same thing to me because they could
not believe that this product could be so beneficial without either seeing something in writing or seeing the product itself. Fortunately, this is exactly why I am
here. Our company didn't want to just send a piece of paper in the mail. Instead,

they wanted a live person who could interact with you, answer any questions you might have, and provide you with the quality of service you have come to expect."

2. Objection #2: *"I'm not comfortable with buying over the telephone."*

### Identify Why it Occurs

As we have already learned, customers tend to buy something over the telephone only when they are completely comfortable with the person selling the product, or with the industry in general. Perhaps everything about the program sounds good; what is holding the customer back is that the customer doesn't feel secure about performing a transaction over the telephone. In this

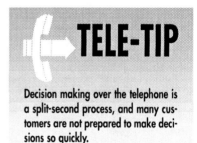

**TELE-TIP**

Decision making over the telephone is a split-second process, and many customers are not prepared to make decisions so quickly.

case, the TSR has to make sure his product is not the issue before tackling the credibility issue.

### Transition Phrase

"I understand completely, Ms. Smith, and before I began my career here, I felt quite the same way you did."

### Handling and Overcoming The Objection

"It's very important to me that you understand everything we are talking about, and that you are comfortable with any decision you make. Based on the fact that I have delivered this product to thousands of customers like you every week, I know that it is very good and very reliable. May I ask, is there something I said about the product that you feel doesn't benefit you?"

3. Objection #3: *"I'm not interested in your product."*

### Identify Why it Occurs

After hearing a presentation, the customer will have one of two reactions. Either he will accept the program on its merits (which almost never happens!) or object to the offer and / or ask a question. This type of objection occurs because the customer didn't hear anything that provided some value to him in the main presentation.

### Transition Phrase

"I understand exactly how you feel Ms. Smith, because at this time I don't want you to accept something you really don't want."

### Handling and Overcoming The Objection

"I realize how wonderful this program can be for you, however, and my objective is merely to answer any questions and resolve any issues you may have about the product. May I ask why you're not interested at this time?"

4. **Objection #4:** *"I don't have the time."*

### Identify Why it Occurs

This may be a valid objection by the customer, in which case the TSR has to establish a time to call back. On the other hand, a customer will often use this objection as an excuse for not talking to the TSR. The objective for the TSR is to identify where the customer is coming from, and then handle it.

### Transition Phrase

"I apologize for calling at a poor time. What time today or tomorrow would be better for me to give you a call back?"

"I understand you are extremely busy, and that's why I can explain everything in just thirty seconds."

### Handling and Overcoming The Objection

"Ms Smith, it's important to me that you have all the time you need to learn everything you can about this product. Before we go, did you find the product interesting and something you might enjoy?" If yes: "Do you have just one minute to spend with me so we can finish discussing the value of the program for you?"

5. **Objection #5:** *"No."*

### Identify Why it Occurs

An objection of "no" usually comes about when the customer is very unclear regarding what the TSR wants from the customer. If this happens early in the presentation, then the customer is saying this to try to ward off the TSR, primarily because the customer is afraid to get involved in a telephone solicitation. If the answer "no" happens after the presentation has been made, in the form of a general objection, it's because the customer is not grasping the benefits of the product, and doesn't want to volunteer the information why. In many instances, the customer doesn't have valid reasons in his mind why he is objecting – his initial reaction is one of lack of interest, so his conditioned response is to just say "no".

### Transition Phrase

"Obviously there is a reason you are not interested."

### Handling and Overcoming The Objection

"In the past, I have been told that my presentation is sometimes unclear. May I ask what I said that turned you away?"

6. **Objection #6:** *"I can't afford"*

### Identify Why it Occurs

Two possible answers. First, the customer legitimately can't afford the product, in which case it's important to break down the actual cost of the product.

Can he not afford the product straight out?

Can he not afford the product based on the value he places on the product?

To combat the price issue, each customer must be qualified appropriately.

**A first objection is the easiest objection to handle, because the first objection is the least meaningful objection.**

Second, the customer may not have an interest in the product, and may be feigning poverty in order to convince the TSR that he should stop presenting and move on to another customer.

## Transition Phrase

"At first glance, I can see that the product looks expensive."

## Handling and Overcoming The Objection

"But when you weigh the price of the program versus the value it will provide to you, I think you'll see how cost-effective it really is. Let me ask you, how much do you think this should cost to become valuable?"

"Why do you believe the price isn't worth the investment?"

"Can you see how the product can be worth its price?"

7. **Objection #7:** *"Let me think it over."*

### Identify Why it Occurs

Decision making over the telephone is a split-second process, and many customers are not prepared to make decisions so quickly. Hence, they choose to think the decision over. In addition, alternative motives exist. For example, the customer may not believe that the offer is worth pursuing, but may not want to explain this fact to the TSR. Or, a spouse or additional decision-maker may need to be contacted before a final decision can be reached, and the customer may want to contact that person first.

### Transition Phrase

"It's important to me that you make the most informed decision."

### Handling and Overcoming The Objection

"May I ask why you want to think it over?"

"Are you interested in the program?"

"Are there one or two elements you are not sure of?"

"What parts of the program did you like the most?"

"Wouldn't you rather make a decision while the information is fresh in your mind?"

8. Objection #8: *"Please send me some literature, instead."*

### Identify Why it Occurs

Customers have a desire to see before they buy, because society has taught us to be secure with what we see, not with what we hear. Literature provides a permanence for the customer. In addition, requesting literature is one of the most common excuses customers use to object to a presentation. Do they really want literature? Possibly.

### Transition Phrase

"Certainly, Ms. Smith, your interest in literature is important."

### Handling and Overcoming The Objection

"What I want to emphasize is that receiving literature isn't enough, because literature can only provide you with the information we want you to read. In addition, it is impossible to ask questions of literature, and it's important that you do ask questions."

"What areas are you looking to read about?"

"What questions do you have that you hope the literature will answer?"

"What information have I not covered?"

"By asking for literature, can I assume that you are interested in our offer?"

"If I send you literature, will you consider joining?"

"I believe receiving literature is a complement to our offer, but it is far more important that you meet with a real person."

## HANDLING AND OVERCOMING THE EARLY OBJECTION

A first objection is the easiest objection to handle, because the first objection is the least meaningful objection. Customers may sound like fierce, angry tigers when they present early objections, but a strong rebuttal can quickly change the whole flow of the conversation. TSRs must understand that early objections are misleading. For example, very inexperienced TSRs find it much easier to give up early and move on to another customer when hearing a preliminary early objection (WRONG!!!), as opposed to actually pursuing that call and trying to make something out of the presentation (RIGHT!!!!!). TSRs must recognize that the difference between a winning presentation and a disappointing presentation may lie in the way the TSR handles that first objection. When the first objection occurs, it is helpful to remember that the objection may have been elicited from the customer by conditioning only. Unlike a customer who hears an entire offer and then offers an objection because he understands the program but is not interested, an <u>early</u> objection usually stems from societal conditioning. Customers object early in the hope that the TSR will give up quickly and everybody can go on their merry way. Early objections include:

**TELE-TIP**

Handling an early objection in the beginning stages of the sales presentation affords the TSR a greater chance of closing the sale than if the customer had not objected at all.

### "Prove to me…"

This objection means the customer doesn't quite believe in the product being offered and needs to hear more information.

### "I don't trust you…"

This objection relates to credibility. When a customer doesn't believe what the TSR is saying, the TSR hasn't demonstrated enough credibility early on to convince the customer, and he offers an objection.

### "I'm not interested…"

This objection, based on conditioning, is expressed when the customer has had too many calls about this subject or too many calls overall and doesn't have the time or patience to hear about the offer. The only way to get the customer's attention is to demonstrate a reason for the customer to continue listening.

### "I don't have the time…"

This could be true, in which case the TSR must establish a time to call back. Often, a customer will use this objection to brush off the sales person, in which case the sales person must be savvy enough to realize this and provide the customer with a convincing rebuttal to allow a presentation to take place.

### "No…"

I always refer to this as my "scaredy cat objection." Early in a presentation the customer can't logically say "no" to an offer without having a reason. Most often, the customer says "no" as a simple and aggressive sum of the previous four early objections. (The customer wants the TSR to prove the product; the customer doesn't believe the TSR has credibility; the customer has been subjected to too many calls and doesn't have the patience for another; the customer doesn't have the time or is looking for an answer to brush the TSR off.) The reasoning behind "no" is very much a product of conditioning and a product of safety. The customer wants to be defensive and protect himself from a presentation.

The way to handle an early objection is to shoot a quick transition phrase to the customer.

### "Prove to me…"

"Ms. Smith, I would be happy to. You know, many other customers have said the exact same thing to me because they couldn't believe that what I was saying could be so beneficial – After I was finished though, they were more than satisfied with this product…"

### "I don't trust you…"

"Believe me Ms. Smith, I don't blame you for being skeptical. It is important before you agree to do anything that I have your full trust and confidence. Otherwise, I would not expect you to, or ask you to, do anything you didn't want to do…"

### "I'm not interested…"

"I understand exactly how you feel Ms. Smith, and that's why I'm not asking you to make any decision right now. I don't want you to accept something you really aren't interested in. Instead, I'm happy to answer any issues you have about the program. May I ask what some of your issues about the program are?"

### "I don't have the time…"

"I realize that you are very busy Ms. Smith. If I could just take 10 seconds of your time, I think you will be very happy to hear what I have to say. If not, I'll call back tomorrow. Which is best for you?"

### "No…"

"Obviously, there is a reason you're not interested. May I ask what I said?"

I believe that handling an early objection in the beginning stages of the sales presentation affords the TSR a greater chance of closing the sale than if the customer had not objected at all, and instead listened to the entire presentation without interruption! My reasoning is simple. When the customer objects early, he is making himself a valuable part of the presentation. Instead of allowing the TSR to talk at him in the hope the customer truly will understand, the customer offers to participate early in the presentation. It is a wonderful opportunity for the TSR to establish rapport.

TSRs also understand that an early objection is what I like to call a "shallow objection." And in sales, handling the shallow aspect of anything is always easy.

**TELE-TIP**

Once later objections take place, the TSR must think close.

A "shallow objection" is an objection from the customer that has no merit or reason behind it. The meat and potatoes are missing from the objection, and because the content of the objection is weak, the TSR's response usually succeeds in allowing the telephone call to continue. As telephone selling continues to become a more saturated and difficult sell in society, more and more "shallow objections" from customers are going to take place as customers begin to attempt to differentiate those sales people who deserve to be heard from those who don't.

## HANDLING AND OVERCOMING LATER OBJECTIONS

As we explore later objections, it is important that we discover exactly why later objections are so difficult to handle and overcome. Indeed, TSRs should consider themselves victorious if they reach the point in a presentation when later objections occur, and even more so if they succeed in handling and overcoming them. To reach later objections, a full presentation has to be made. The introduction, qualification, probing, benefits and features, and trial closing aspects of the presentation all must be completed. Then a later objection takes place to spoil a perfectly good sales presentation.

Why are later objections so difficult to handle and overcome? *First*, later objections are by-products of a tough customer and a persistent sales person. This means that the customer has not been easily swayed into buying and still has objections; it also means that the TSR is persistent, but is nevertheless unable to close. By definition, later objections are tough to overcome because two equally challenging foes are going head-to-head. The customer is sending out valid objections that are stopping him from saying "yes," and the TSR is returning the volley with fantastic rebuttals that are convincing the customer to stay on the line and continue being a part of the conversation. It is as if two equally matched wrestlers are battling in a match that nobody can win. *Second*, later objections become difficult to handle and overcome because many of the TSR's best benefits and features have already been presented. What is left? *Third*, later objections mean the customer hasn't been sold, and the longer the customer remains in the conversation saying "no" and providing objections, the more "no conditioning" is taking affect. Eventually, the customer will be so conditioned to say "no" that he will refuse under any circumstances to be swayed by the TSR and to say "yes."

## HOW TO HANDLE AND OVERCOME LATE OBJECTIONS

● **Don't Stop Pursuing**

TSRs must maintain the mindset that customers who offer objections are doing what they are supposed to do. When customers offer objections, they are playing their game extremely well, so the TSR must begin also to play the game well by getting them to do what the TSR wants them to do. Once the TSR lets up, the sales call is finished, because the customer is never going to give in. As long as the presentation has reached the later stages, the TSR can't stop until every rock has been overturned.

● **Continue To Ask Questions, Questions, Questions That Involve The Customer**

Questions are the key. We know that. Questions draw out answers that help the TSR, as well as provide an outlet for the prospect. In the beginning of a conversation, questions may be deemed too pushy or sales oriented. By the time of the later objections, questions are the continuation of a rapport that has already been established.

"May I ask what specific concerns you may have?"

"Which questions have I not answered for you?"

"I understand that you want to think about it, and that's important to me because it shows me that you really are interested. What areas are you planning to think about?"

"I don't quite understand. Can you clarify for me?"

"Tell me a little bit about_____"

● **Redirect The Customer's Objections Through Questions**

Perhaps the greatest way to handle and overcome an objection is to answer the objection with a question of the TSR's own. In addition, TSRs should not only ask questions of their own, but they should redirect the objection they just heard through the question. This does a few things for the TSR and the customer. *First*, it proves to the customer that the TSR is paying attention. *Second*, it proves to the customer that the TSR wants to deal directly with the objection at hand. *Third*, it throws the objection right back at the customer, and builds conversation. Now, instead of forcing the TSR to answer the objection, the TSR is encouraging the customer to talk more about his own objection, and provide more information which the TSR might be able to use.

CUSTOMER:  "I'm really very happy."

TSR:       "I understand you're happy. What is it about your program that makes you happy?"

CUSTOMER:  "I've worked with the same company for ten years and I'm not changing."

TSR:       "You've been with them for ten years? Why did you originally go with them?"

CUSTOMER:  "Changing is too much trouble, and it isn't the right time for us."

TSR:       "It's not the right time?"

CUSTOMER:  "Too expensive."

TSR:         "I tend to agree, at first glance it would appear to be expensive. How much would you pay for a product like this?"

CUSTOMER:  "I need to think about it."

TSR:         "You need to think about it? Why?"

## ● Sense When The Conversation Is Stagnant And Change It

Nobody wants a boring or stagnant conversation, and it is the job of the TSR to sense when the conversation has become boring or stagnant. The old adage is that "Everybody likes the life of a party." Well, if there is no life in a telephone sales party, the TSR needs to generate some life, quick.

## ● Emphasize Sincerity and Desire

As I have touched upon in various portions of this book, I believe wholeheartedly that the customer buys the TSR as well as the program on nearly every call. Taking this a step further, later objection usually means that the customer has some sense of comfort with both the TSR and the program. The TSR must not overplay his hand by losing the sincerity or desire he once demonstrated to this customer earlier in the call. The customer will sense quickly if he is wearing down the TSR, and the TSR doesn't want to give the customer that opportunity. Clearly, sincerity and desire build the rapport that allows the TSR to battle late objections.

## ● Motivate the Decision Making Process

The main difference between early objections and later objections is that TSRs need to be more patient with early objections and more motivational with later objections. After an early objection, the TSR is most concerned with gaining direction of the call, establishing a credible relationship, finding out the customer's needs, and developing a presentation that will sell the appropriate benefits. After a later objection, all of that has already been done. At that point, the chance to close the sale rests solely in the TSR's ability to motivate the customer. How can a TSR do this? *First*, create the finishing line. Point out where the telephone call is going and where it has been by utilizing themes, images and concepts. If the customer feels there is an end zone ahead, he will be more likely to focus on it. *Second*, overwhelm the customer with sincerity. Human nature dictates that people want to do well by other people. Some of the best TSRs are those who emphasize that they, too, are a part of the closing process. The customer may be purchasing a product, but he is also investing his time and money in the sales representative who helped him buy that product.

## ● Sell Pertinent Benefits and Features That Directly Appeal to The Customer

When handling later objections, not just any run-of-the-mill benefit or feature will do the trick. Customers are looking for motivation at this stage, not generalities, and they are looking for specific motivations for their specific desires. Most likely the customer will have heard quite a few benefits and features already, enough to maintain the customer's motivation to stay around and object, so the emphasis when selling benefits and features at this stage is to sell only <u>appropriate ones</u>.

How does the TSR find the appropriate benefits and features? By asking questions, and hearing intently what the answers to these questions are. Utilizing hearing skills is critical here. Then, the TSR can take four paths to precisely sell the appropriate benefits and features when the customer objects at the later stage of the sales cycle. *First,* it is important that the TSR keep his explanation of the benefits and features very brief. After the customer has reached this later stage, he understands that the TSR is trying to convince him to make a positive decision, and it is meat and potatoes that will often sway the customer. Time and information overload also become factors. The TSR must keep the explanation short for maximum impact. *Second,* the TSR need only repeat those benefits and features that were successful in the general presentation. In most instances, the benefits and features used in the general presentation didn't work, because if they had, the customer probably would not have provided later objections. Rehashing those benefits and features that didn't work will not persuade the customer to accept an offer, even if the TSR feels that those benefits and features are his strongest. Too often, I have heard TSRs handle later objections by rehashing very inconsequential benefits and features, and this is a common error. <u>But if a benefit or feature truly motivated the customer to appreciate a product early on in the presentation, it becomes mandatory when handling later objections that the TSR utilize this fact to increase the chances of the customer saying "yes."</u> Very often, customers forget how much they liked something ten or fifteen minutes earlier, because they dislike so much more what they have just heard. The TSR can't assume the customer remembers an early benefit. He must express it again. *Third,* the TSR must present only one or two benefits and features, and then stop and begin the trial closing process. The mistake many TSRs make is that they rattle off six or seven quality benefits in a row to the customer, in order to try to persuade the customer to accept them. Unfortunately, after hearing one or two benefits, the impact of the rest are lost on the customer, because the customer is not mentally capable of taking in so much information at one time. Illustrating one or two benefits and features will provide the maximum quality impact to close the sale. *Fourth,* the TSR must be cognizant to provide as dynamic and lively a sell of his benefits and features as possible. Description when handling late objections can make or break the sale. Benefits and features must have pizzazz!!…zip!!..pow!! They need to grasp the customer and say "I am something you must have, and you must want it now!" By using images, themes and concepts to his advantage, the TSR can paint a valuable picture to the customer.

● **Trial Close And Close; Trial Close And Close; Keep Closing**

Once later objections take place, the TSR must think close. In the beginning of the presentation, the TSR doesn't think close, and at the end of the presentation, the TSR doesn't think about qualifying for basic needs. Thus, later objections are high time for closing. The most effective way for the TSR to accomplish this is to trial close the customer, receive affirmation, and then close. The key to handling later objections is that the TSR must constantly close. Anything less than trying to put a stamp of approval on the presentation will result in the customer's continuing objections.

"You said you wanted the bags in green, right? Well, I have 1,000 bags ready to ship to you, and they are all in green. How does that sound?"

"What did you say was more important to you, money or fun? I agree, and because we can provide you with 100% more fun, isn't it best that we get started now?"

## CONCLUSION

TSRs tend to think of objection as rejection, when in fact they should focus on the fact that rejection is personal and final, and objection is casual with the opportunity to effect change. By understanding why customers object, the game of handling and overcoming objection becomes much easier to play. By being educated and then by putting into practice the steps and philosophies of handling objection, TSRs can increase their success rate in overcoming objection. Handling objection is very much a psychological game. Certainly, objections sting. Yet the very reason a presentation is successful is because the customer felt strongly enough about something (the TSR, the product, an interest) to stay around and offer objections.

# *Appendix*

On the following pages are three sample telephone sales presentations. The purpose of enclosing these presentations in <u>Friendly Persuasion</u> is to provide the reader with general examples of how a telephone sales presentation can take place, following the steps of this book and incorporating the subject most utilized as an example: selling children's books. All telephone sales presentations are different, and one similar quality all three of these have are that they are short and to the point. These examples have not been developed to provide the reader with the usual standard, run-of-the-mill chatter and banter that fills up time and space in a presentation. Every TSR recognizes that chatter and banter and "fill time" will always exist. Instead, the three sample telephone presentations were designed to focus on the critical aspects of the telephone sales presentation, so the reader could see directly how telephone selling exists as we head into the 21st century.

## SAMPLE PRESENTATION #1

A.

"Hello, this is Howard McDowell and I am calling from the Children's Books Store. Can I speak to the person who purchases books in your home?" (**Introduction**)

"Yes, that's me."

B.

"Good morning. Our records indicate that you have an interest in fine children's books, and that you have purchased books and magazines for your children in the past. Is that correct?" (**Qualifying**)

"Yes."

C.

"Great. The purpose of my call is to interest you in trying out a set of six children's books, especially designed for children like yours. They are easy to read, wonderful learning tools and an exceptional value. Does that sound good?"

(**Benefits** **Trial Close**)

"Yes."

D.

"Fantastic. Let me confirm your order?"
(**Close**)

"Right now we're not interested. Thank you for calling."

E.

"I understand exactly how you feel. Ms / Mr._____. It's important to note that these exceptional children's books are on sale for only $49.99. Let's get you started…"
(**Handle Objection** **Close**)

"I'm not interested, because we have more than enough children's books."

F.

"True, but at the same time you don't receive anywhere near the quality you would receive with our product. We guarantee to provide more value than our competitor. So, while their initial purchase may be less expensive, you will end up not receiving nearly the value you would receive with us. Does that make sense?"
(**Handle Objection** **Trial Close**)

"Yes."

G.

"Clearly, we will be much more cost effective for you in the long run. Do you agree?"
(**Trial Close**)

"Yes."

H.

"Great. Let's get started."
(**Close**)

"Okay."

## SAMPLE PRESENTATION #2

A.

"Hello, Ms./ Mr._____? Hi, my name is Howard McDowell and I am calling from the Children's Books Store. How are you today?"
(**Introduction**)

"I'm doing well, thank you."

B.

"Wonderful. The reason for my call is that we've identified you, and your children, as a family that might be interested in learning about and enjoying quality children's books. I was wondering, do you presently have children in the house?"
(**Qualifying**)

"Yes, I do."

C.

"May I ask how many you have and how old they are?"
(**Qualifying**)

"Right now I have two. One boy who is eight, one girl who is six."

D.

"I imagine that is quite a handful. Do they read many children's books?"
(**Probe**)

"They do, although the boy doesn't read as much as the girl. He seems to be running around all of the time or watching television."

E.

"Well, I guess that's how boys, and girls, are. I have two kids who are a bit older, and they were the same way. Out of curiosity, what types of books are they reading?"
(**Rapport**       Probe)

"Well, my girl is focusing on all of the stories we all grew up with, such as Snow White, Cinderella and all of those. As for my son, he likes the science fiction more than anything else."

F.

"Well, I'll tell you why I called, and I feel you will be interested in this. Our children's book store offers tremendous books for boys and girls under thirteen years old, and we've been doing so for many years. We have all of the stories and subjects you mentioned, plus many others, and we're making our offer available to families like yours. How do you usually purchase books for your kids?"
(**Benefits and Features**       Probe)

"We've only bought books at the bookstore."

G.

"Everybody I talk to says the same thing, but believe it or not, we've provided over 10,000 sets of books to children all across the country using the telephone. For a one time charge of $29.99, we send you six quality, hardback, durable books for your son or daughter to enjoy. If they aren't completely satisfied within thirty days, you can return the books and we will refund your money. It's really that simple. Can you see how starting an order can be truly beneficial for your children?"
(**Handle built in objection**       **Sell program**       **Trial Close**)

"It sounds interesting, and I do see some advantages, but I'm going to have to think it over."

H.

"I understand how you feel, and as I've said, most people have felt quite the same way, at first. Let me ask, what are the things about this program that you want to think about?"
(**Handle Objection**       Probe)

"Well, you hit it on the head. I have never ordered books over the telephone before, and it would be nice if I could see them before I make a decision."

I.

"Ms / Mr._____, let's look at our offer this way. Although you never had the good opportunity to order books over the telephone, many more of your peers have and found it very beneficial to them and their children. That's why we offer a trial period so you and your child can sit down, review the books together, and then decide whether you want to keep them, or send them back. In any event, the obligation is to enjoy the books and decide, not decide and pay a penalty."
(**Handle Objection**)

"It sounds good, but I'm not sure I feel comfortable paying for the books over the telephone."

J.

"I don't blame you at all, I feel the same way when I make purchases over the telephone. What we do is send you an invoice after you decide to keep the books, and you can return that invoice with a check, and we'll pick up the postage. The important thing is that you don't have to pay now. We feel so strongly that your children will enjoy these books that we only ask for payment after you've completely accepted them. Let's get the order out today. Are you still located at………"
(**Handle Objection          Close**)

## SAMPLE PRESENTATION #3

A.

"Hello, may I please speak to Ms./ Mr._____?"
"May I tell them who is calling?"

B.

"Yes. Let them know my name is Howard McDowell, and I'm calling on behalf of the Children's Books Store."

C.

"Hello, Ms / Mr_____. My name is Howard McDowell and I am calling from the Children's Books Store. How are you today?"
(**Introduction**)

"I'm doing well, thank you. What do you need?"

D.

"I'll be brief. The reason for my call is that we've identified you, and your children, as a family that might be interested in learning about and enjoying quality children's books. I was wondering, do you presently have children in the house?"
(**Qualifying**)

"Yes, I do, but I don't think we'll be interested."

E.

"I understand exactly how you feel, Mr. /Ms_____, because many of my best customers said the same exact thing the first time I called them. Even though you have no interest right now, I think you will find what I have to say incredibly interesting. May I ask how many children you have and how old they are?"
(**Handle Early Objection          Qualifying**)

"Well, we have two, ages eight and six. They're not much into reading though, so I don't think I'm going to be interested."

F.

"To be honest, most of the parents I speak with say their children aren't big readers at that age, so that's quite alright. In fact, that's one of the reasons why I think these books may be perfect for them. Our children's books store offers tremendous books for boys and girls under thirteen years old, and we've been doing so for many years. These books increase learning skills, add enjoyment to reading, and open up whole new worlds for children like yours. Have you given much thought to enrolling them in a book program?"
(**Handle Objection          Sell Benefits          Probe**)

"None at all. How much is this going to cost me?"

G.

'Mr/Ms_____, for a one-time charge of $29.99, we send you six quality, hardback, durable books for your son or daughter to enjoy. If they aren't completely satisfied within thirty days, you can return the books and we will refund your money. It's really that simple. Can you see how starting an order can be truly beneficial for your children?"
(**Handle Question**      **Sell program**      **Trial Close**)

"I'm going to have to think it over."

H.

"I understand how you feel, and as I've said, most people have felt quite the same way, at first. Let me ask, what are the things about this program that you really liked?"
(**Handle Objection**      **Probe**)

"I think it's important my children understand reading, and I've had trouble getting them involved in reading in the past."

I.

"That's a perfect reason to look at our program. When you join, the books come directly to your house, and the fun and excitement for your kids is partly in seeing the books all wrapped up, and having fun opening them up. Perhaps this will be the first time they truly enjoy seeing books. Don't you agree this is certainly a unique way of receiving books?"
(**Handle Answer**      **Trial Close**)

"Yes."

J.

"Let's get you started. Are you still located at…"
(**Close**)

## ABOUT THE AUTHOR

Dan Coen is a call center executive who has spent years perfecting the art of managing, motivating and training call center agents and staff. He is an expert in developing and cultivating teams in the call center environment, having created and implemented many innovative employee involvement programs. Dan's contribution to the world of telesales and customer service includes conference speeches, employee workshops and published articles in SalesDoctors.Com Magazine, Selling Power Magazine; Teleprofessional Magazine; Call

Center Magazine; Service Level Newsletter; and Telephone Selling Report. His second book Influencing Call Center Supervisors and Agents is due out next year.

P.O. Box 571533
Tarzana, CA 91357
Orders: 888-835-5326
Fax /Direct Line: 818-703-1022
DcdDcd@aol.com

## Don't Forget To Order These Other Products From DCD Publishing

*Friendly Persuasion*
THE WORKBOOK . . . . . . . . . . . . . . . . . . . . . . . . . . . . $16.00 plus $5.00 S/H
Perfect companion piece to the book
Each section can be used as a sales program to train your call center staff
A refresher workbook for you and your sales team to use over and over again
*Available Now!*

*Influencing Call Center Supervisors And Agents* . . . . $24.50 plus $5.00 S/H
Managing Customer Service And Telesales Personnel To
Break Records In Your Call Center
*Available March, 2000*

*Influencing Call Center Supervisors And Agents* . . . . $16.00 plus $5.00 S/H
THE WORKBOOK
*Available March, 2000*